COLLECTING COSTUME

The Care and Display of Clothes and Accessories

COLLECTING COSTUME

The Care and Display of Clothes and Accessories

NAOMI TARRANT

London
GEORGE ALLEN & UNWIN
Boston   Sydney

George Allen & Unwin (Publishers) Ltd,
40 Museum Street, London WC1A 1LU, UK

George Allen & Unwin (Publishers) Ltd,
Park Lane, Hemel Hempstead, Herts HP2 4TE, UK

Allen & Unwin Inc.,
9 Winchester Terrace, Winchester, Mass 01890, USA

George Allen & Unwin Australia Pty Ltd,
8 Napier Street, North Sydney, NSW 2060, Australia

First published in 1983

British Library Cataloguing in Publication Data
Tarrant, Naomi
    Collecting costume.
    1. Costume – Collectors and collecting
    I. Title
    391'.075   GT511
    ISBN 0-04-746017-2

Set in 10 on 12 point Palatino by
Rowland Phototypesetting Ltd, Bury St Edmunds, Suffolk
and printed in Great Britain by
Butler & Tanner Ltd, Frome and London

In memory of my Mother,
Annie Davies Tarrant

Contents

Illustrations

PHOTOGRAPHIC ACKNOWLEDGEMENTS

Crown Copyright 1, 2, 4, 5–26, 30, 31, 33–35, 38; City of Manchester Art Galleries 3, 36, 37, 39; Museum of London 27; Museum of the City of New York 28, 29; National Trust 2; Worthing Museum and Art Gallery 32.

Preface

This book aims to be a practical manual for the costume collector. It is based on the author's experience of working with costume and textiles in museums for nearly twenty years and is thus an adaptation of museum practices suitable for the private collector. There are some things, though, that can never be passed on through the pages of a book. One of these is the joy of collecting, which the collector will discover for herself.

The photographs have been chosen to illustrate certain points rather than to be a decorative or chronological view of costume history. They are mostly unpublished and from a largely unknown collection which it has been my privilege to curate for the past eight years.

My debts to various friends and colleagues over the years are far too numerous to mention in detail, but I would particularly like to thank past and present colleagues at Chester, Aylesbury, London and Edinburgh. I should also like to thank Janet Arnold for her advice and encouragement, Helen and Philip Bennett for many stimulating discussions (and delicious meals), Charles Stewart for his entertaining stories of costume collecting, Margaret Swain for her northern good sense and hospitality which always revives a flagging spirit, and to the best of parents for always being gently encouraging. Two people who have helped to make the book a reality also deserve my thanks: John Newth of George Allen & Unwin, for his initial interest and unfailing tact; and Antony Kamm, for his wise advice.

All photographs of Royal Scottish Museum objects are Crown Copyright and except for nos 6, 15 and 19–23 are by Ken Smith.

NAOMI TARRANT

PUBLISHER'S NOTE

For convenience, the collector in the singular has been referred to as 'she' throughout the book.

CHAPTER ONE

The survival rate in costume and textiles

'Costume' is the term now generally applied to all types of clothing whether everyday, ceremonial, fancy, folk or theatrical, which have been worn in the past. It is not accepted by some purists who prefer to use dress' for what people wear every day and would reserve costume for theatrical and fancy dress, but most collections of clothing contain a little of all types and costume is a more comprehensive term. 'Clothes' or 'clothing' would be more explicit for the layman but would lead to confusion with our own wearing apparel.

With the clothes go the accessories: hats, handbags, shoes, stockings, handkerchiefs, gloves, fans, parasols and all those dozens of little items that the well-dressed person has always needed. When we dress we create a total picture, and make-up and hairstyles should also be taken into account.

Added to this list of what constitutes costume are the textiles that garments and accessories are made from – often beautiful in their own right and very collectable. These include lace and embroidery as well as fine silks and printed cottons.

Old costumes are usually made from natural fibres (cotton, silk, linen, wool), fur or leather, but in the last hundred years artificial or man-made fibres (rayon, nylon, polyester) have been introduced. These two types of fibre have different properties which affect the survival rate of the costumes made from them.

All natural fibres will decay and start to do so from the moment they are picked or cut because they are the dead products of plants and animals. Man-made fibres are created from either animal or natural products like the cellulose found in plants (rayon), or from mineral products (nylon, polyester).

Although there is no steady measurable deterioration factor applicable to natural fibres, it is, nevertheless, a relentless process and cannot be reversed or halted, only slowed down a little. Some man-made fibres could, in theory, last for ever but as they are produced as a commercial enterprise the makers are not interested in producing indestructible fabrics.

The deterioration rate of fabrics is accelerated by light, dust, dirt, grease, water, dryness and various insects. So, to escape these hazards, costume should be stored in a dark place, not too hot or too cold, not too dry or too damp, and protected from insects. Nor should it be worn or displayed. Costume is quite simply a mass of decaying matter which poses a serious conservation problem for both private and public collections.

To help understand why these conditions of storage are necessary let us look at what happens to the original fibres after they are picked from plants or cut from animals. These fibres are not in a suitable condition for immediate use. Some of the processes they go through to become fabrics are very drastic and it is surprising any survive at all. Only silk can be used virtually untouched from the cocoon, while flax, for example, has to be soaked for days to rot the stems so that the usable fibres can be removed. Wool has to be carded to straighten out the fibres before a long, continuous yarn can be produced.

The next process is spinning which produces a continuous yarn long enough to use in weaving. Because silk was produced as a continuous thread by the caterpillar to make its cocoon it does not need to be spun. Spinning also produces the twist in fibres. To make heavier yarns one or two can be twisted together, that is plied. The fineness of the yarn produced depends on the skill of the spinner and the requirements of the weaver.

The weaver produces the cloth on a loom by crossing two sets of threads at right angles to each other so that they interlock to form a solid fabric. The action of the loom places great strain on the main vertical threads, the warp, and there is friction too, caused by the passing backwards and forwards of the shuttle which holds the horizontal threads, the weft. The warp threads, therefore, have to be very strong to take this kind of treatment, even for sheer fabrics. If a thread is not strong then it will break in the weaving process which will make for uneven cloth.

Either before weaving or afterwards the fibres or fabric will be dyed or bleached. In the past dyes were obtained mainly from vegetable products and the fabric usually had to be boiled in the dye vat for several hours to achieve the strength of colour required. Vegetable dyes are not permanent nor are they very fast in strong sunlight, while the chemical ingredients used can also affect the cloth. Iron was added to the black dye to make it take, but the iron rotted through the fibres and in old embroideries, for example, the black threads will often have rotted away, leaving only the needle holes to show where the threads were. On printed fabrics the outlines were often done in black and sometimes there are lines of holes showing where the fibres have decayed.

From about 1860 onwards dyes began to be synthesised; the chemical ingredients in the dyes were isolated from mineral products, and vegetable dyes were no longer used commercially. But the effects of these synthesised dyes can also be harmful to fibres and the dyeing process is no less strenuous for the fabrics. The tints of modern dyes may be superior but the long-term life expectancy of the fabric is not necessarily improved.

After dyeing and weaving many kinds of finishing processes are used on fabrics. These finishes, which are much more common today, were used in the past to enhance the appearance of the cloth. Sometimes, as in the dressing designed to bulk out cheaper cotton fabrics, they could deceive the customer into thinking the quality was better than it really was.

The most notorious dressing which the costume collector will encounter is that given to silks at the end of the nineteenth and the beginning of the twentieth centuries. Various ingredients were used to weight, or dress, the fabrics, including metal salts. They were often overweighted which caused the severe deterioration seen in these materials. The dressing was used particularly on silk taffetas made into dress linings and petticoats which gave that lovely rustle to the dresses of the 1890s and 1900s, but it can also be found on the satins and silks produced for wedding and evening dresses. The state of these silks is recognised by the severe splitting along the warp, which in the worst cases reduces the fabric to a crumbling mess. It is known as shattered silk and there is no remedy.

But even when it leaves the factory ill treatment of fabric continues. In shops the rolls of cloth are subjected to fingering by the customers, to dust and to light. Then at the tailors or dressmakers the fabric is cut and pinned, gathered and pleated and steamed into shape, using a whole range of mechanical and hand processes which add their own strains.

When the garment is worn there are further hazards to the fabric: perspiration, dirty seats, smoke-filled rooms and food and drink stains. Cleaning with a variety of powders and liquids is also dangerous, or, worse still, neglecting to wash or clean dirty clothes which allows insects to eat the cloth. It is surprising that anything survives these hazards, and yet the quantity of costume which remains in Britain is immense.

It is also vital to protect textiles, especially old textiles, from light, and this is the single most controversial issue when displaying costume because the invariable complaint from the public is that the clothes cannot be seen properly. Most people realise from their own experience that light fades colours, but light also attacks the fibres that make up the fabrics so that they become brittle and break. This is not as visibly dramatic as fading but it takes place nevertheless. So every time an item is displayed, no matter how dim the light, some harm is being done to it.

Dust and dirt contain small particles of grit which, in time, will cut the fibres, so it is important to keep dirt well away from the clothes and to see that any already there is brushed off. Grease and food stains can be very difficult to remove once they have become fixed in the cloth without the use of harsh cleaning agents, and these in turn can affect the dyes or make holes or permanent spots in the fabric. Grease attracts dust and food stains can encourage insect and other animal life. These creatures, in the process of eating the food, will make holes in the fabric. Mice are also a problem as they will nibble anything soft from which to make nests.

Water can mark fabrics and cause dyes to run thus making ugly stains and, together with heat, provides the right conditions for mould to grow. Alternatively, dryness can make the fibres too brittle so that they break because the water content, necessary for suppleness, is removed.

Even the careful wearing of costume should be discouraged since too much washing, even by a trained conservator, is not good for the garments. Each time they are handled some harm is being done. Dry cleaning is a harsher treatment often involving some mechanical action, and although it is sometimes the only practical step it is never advisable to repeat this treatment. So once a costume has been cleaned it should be well stored.

CHAPTER TWO

Types of costume available

Very few people sit down and make the conscious decision to collect a particular type of object. Most just wake up one day to the fact that they have the basis of a collection and it goes on from there. At that point, however, it is a good idea to step back, take a look at the collection and ask a few pertinent questions.

The collector should first ask herself why she is collecting – for her job, for pleasure, to satisfy an urge or because it is fashionable to collect something? There is something of the squirrel in most people and collecting is certainly a major modern hobby, but it is as well to choose something which is enjoyable and in the case of costume you must like it enough to have patience with its demands.

Costume that is used for practical purposes will, of course, be very vulnerable. An art teacher with a course in the history of dress to teach, or a teacher in a school where objects form an important part of the lessons, will use their collections in a way that makes them a wasting asset. The pieces will not survive tough handling for too long. Designers who wish to build up their own reference collection of costumes will determine its life expectancy by the use that they give it and the way it is handled and stored.

If you want to collect for a hobby, and have taken into account what has been said on the physical aspects of fabrics, there are one or two important points to realise if you do not want to end up with a collection of rags. In the first place storage is very important, secondly a collection needs a great deal of good housekeeping, and thirdly it is not something which can be displayed easily or shown off to friends in the way that glass or porcelain can.

What is collected depends on why the collection is being made. The emphasis of a collection built up for reference may well vary from that of one which is made as a hobby. You can add to the enjoyment of collecting if you specialise and this also helps if space is a problem, and do not forget that complete dresses take up more space than accessories. Flat textiles are easier to store than three-dimensional clothes, while parasols are probably the most difficult accessory to store properly. Many people already collect fans, lace, buttons, button-hooks and samplers and there are specialist books and societies to help them.

To give a complete rundown on the different types of costume with prices is impractical because the fluctuations in the market make this type of information out of date as soon as it is printed. Unlike porcelain, for example, clothes were not factory products mass produced over a number of years, but were nearly always individually made until the present century, and even couture garments varied from client to client as each one had some personal touch added. For this reason the comparison of one piece with another is not practical. Personal preferences are also important; you may dislike pink, for instance, and would not wish to pay a high price for a pink dress, but would do so for a black one. But it is possible to give a summary of the various types of garments and their general availability at present.

EUROPEAN FASHIONABLE DRESS

Baby clothes

These are abundant because babies had large trousseaux in the nineteenth century. You can build up a good collection of babywear from the mid-nineteenth century to the present at a fairly low cost. The most difficult items to find will be those of the last fifty years because of the modern tendency to dispose of items which are no longer needed.

The beautiful embroidered long clothes, usually called christening robes today, are particularly attractive and very plentiful. Most museums no longer accept these unless the garment has belonged to a well-known local figure. Together with small caps, these robes were produced in vast quantities, notably by the embroideresses of Ayrshire and Northern Ireland, between about 1830 and 1860. Later examples were often in 'broderie anglaise', a whitework embroidery with eyelet holes, but the type was still being made into this century,

1   Detail of baby's long-clothes of fine white cotton embroidered with the whitework known as Ayrshire, about 1830. The delicate needle-lace fillings of the holes are a distinctive feature of this work. Signs of stress can appear on the area round the satin stitch and in the fillings, noticeable in this example, and great care has to be taken during washing. *Royal Scottish Museum, 1952.1*

though with much less embroidery and more contemporary motifs. These gowns are still used for present-day christenings.

Children's wear

This is much more difficult to find because of the poor survival rate of children's clothes. In large families clothes were handed down to the younger children and the heavy wear they received tended to increase with the child's age. Toddlers' clothes are less rare comparatively than those for school-age children, but teenagers' wear is difficult to come across because some adult-sized clothes may well belong to them. It is possible to identify debutante evening dresses occasionally, though the whole area of mid- to late-teenage clothing is a problem and one that has received little attention from researchers.

Prices of children's clothes are now high for anything other than the white toddlers' dresses dating from the beginning of this century.

Women's underwear

This is another reasonably priced field for nineteenth-century examples. Some pieces such as crinoline cages and corsets can be expensive, but in general white chemises, nightdresses, camisoles, petticoats and drawers are readily available. There is sometimes competition whenever there is a vogue for using these items as fashion garments, as in the recent craze for Victorian nightdresses and petticoats. But there are a vast number of these clothes about and it should be possible to find them quite cheaply.

It is harder to find the very pretty crêpe-de-chine pieces which were the expensive lingerie of the 1920s and 1930s. These were often produced in sets and are delicate, which makes their survival less likely than the fairly stout white long-cloth of the previous century. Again there can be competition from the fashion trade for these items and when found they will not be cheap.

It is very rare to find any underwear dated earlier than the mid-nineteenth century, apart from eighteenth-century corsets which seem to survive better, no doubt because they are formidable pieces, heavily boned and not easily destroyed.

Women's dresses

This is the largest and probably the most popular collecting field, but anything dating from the eighteenth century will be too expensive for most new collectors, unless it is in a very bad state of preservation. In addition nearly all eighteenth-century dresses have been altered, either shortly after they were originally made to keep pace with changing fashion, or in the nineteenth century for fancy dress. Unless she knows what to look for the collector could well spend a lot of money on a dress which has been very badly remade as a nineteenth-century fancy dress.

All nineteenth-century dresses of good quality which are unaltered now fetch high prices, the most expensive probably being those from the 1820s onwards to the 1890s. The quantity of dresses surviving from the period between about 1890 and 1914 makes this the cheapest area for good dresses. However, sale prices are always unpredictable where attractive items are concerned and it only needs two people to want the same dress and the price will soar.

The easiest items to collect are those from the twentieth century, especially from the 1920s and 1930s. Beaded evening dresses from the 1920s are abundant, but again suffer from being bought up to

2 A group of figures illustrating a wedding party of *c.* 1900 in a country-house drawing room, wearing a range of clothes from this period. The figures have papier-mâché heads with stylised features. *The National Trust, Killerton House, nr Exeter*

wear. Evening dresses are generally more plentiful than day clothes although it is possible to build a fine and attractive collection from this period.

A large number of 1950s and 1960s items are now finding their way onto the market, many of them from the ready-to-wear sections of the well-known Parisian couture houses. The collector would be well advised to check which label was used in the cheaper ready-to-wear clothes as opposed to those of the main couture house, as they were usually designed not by the chief designer but by his assistants.

Collectors should be wary of going for the big name labels. The current favourites are Fortuny, Chanel, Poiret and others of the 1920s and 1930s. This interest has raised the prices for their clothes as you would expect. It was not unusual in America before 1914 for manufacturers to forge labels in dresses, pretending they came from a well-known Parisian house, and although this is not recorded in Britain it is something to be aware of.

Because there is so much available in this range of clothes it is a good idea to specialise in a particular decade or type of garment. This might make the hunt more difficult but it will certainly add to your enjoyment.

Women's outer wear

Coats are a relatively late introduction for women. Before the early nineteenth century, when short jackets called spencers and long coats called pelisses were popular, the usual outdoor garment was a cape or cloak, but it is rare to find these today. Other types of outer wear are flat textiles and will be discussed later. Various lace and net jackets appeared in the 1850s but it is really in the 1870s that heavy jackets and coats became popular. Travelling capes of heavy tweed are occasionally found but coats only really became widespread in the 1920s and most of the surviving garments date from then onwards.

The tailor-made suit is really classified under dresses because the finest examples were worn in town and not in the country. The classic country tweed suit is rarely found for any period.

Men's clothes

Men's clothes survive in far fewer numbers than women's. Underwear, which consisted basically of a shirt and some form of underpants and a nightshirt, was never as numerous as that worn by

3 An afternoon dress and coat of about 1925. The coat is of silk with a fur collar and is worn with a felt cloche hat, bar shoes, thick lisle stockings and a small pochette handbag. *The Gallery of English Costume, Platt Hall, Manchester*

women, and it would be very difficult to collect a range of men's underwear from the eighteenth century to the present. Although the prices are usually not too high when they do come on the market, it is only occasionally that they appear.

Complete suits are very rare. The beautifully embroidered ones of the eighteenth century, if found intact, are extremely expensive. Single coats are much commoner and cheaper.

Nineteenth-century suits are just as hard to find. Again, coats without trousers tend to survive, although the linen trousers worn in summer are fairly common. Evening and morning suits of the late nineteenth and twentieth centuries can be found complete.

The items of the male wardrobe which are found in the largest numbers are waistcoats and you could get together a good collection of these from the mid-eighteenth century onwards at a reasonable cost. They also have the advantage of being easier to store than many of the larger items. Anyone also interested in embroidery would find these attractive and the wide range of materials used adds interest to them as a collector's item.

Civil uniform

This is worn by non-military men at Court for special occasions such as drawing rooms and levées, held by the sovereign for the presentation of people in public life. The plain velvet Court suit in the new style, that is cut like a modern tail coat, and dating from this century, is the most numerous survivor. Anyone with a government post had to wear a style of outfit more like a uniform,

4 Men's accessories as follows: a pair of black evening shoes sold by Harrods between the wars; a handkerchief with a small printed decoration dated 1863; a white muslin stock, early nineteenth century; a moustache trainer to wear at night, about 1880–90. *Royal Scottish Museum, 1975.406&A; 1978.408; 1914.272F; 1967.176*

5 A man's Court suit of mulberry-coloured cloth trimmed with cut steel buttons and worn with an embroidered white silk waistcoat, white silk stockings, black shoes and with a black chapeau-bras carried under the arm, British, about 1820. This style of Court suit was worn throughout most of the nineteenth century with black velvet gradually predominating. There is a black silk wig-bag sewn to the back of the collar and this purely decorative feature was worn with this style until the end. Cut steel buttons usually denote a Court suit.

This figure had thighs that were too thick for the breeches and they were replaced by steel rods. The shoes are genuine but had been mutilated in the past by having a hole bored through one sole. The base plate, into which the spike under the foot is slotted, is hidden under the carpet. *Royal Scottish Museum, 1892.566*

consisting of a blue cloth coat with varying amounts of gold embroidery down the front, the most elaborate ones being worn only by privy councillors. These are expensive today as the collectors of militaria have become interested in them. Items such as lords lieutenants' or ambassadors' outfits are not found as frequently as the Court suits.

Accessories

Shoes. These are now commanding rather high prices at sales, no doubt because there is competition between collectors. Anything pre-1890, other than the very common women's satin, ballet-style evening shoes, are probably now beyond the pockets of the modest collector. Nineteenth-century shoes with a maker's label, especially those of little-known or provincial makers, will cost you more. Post-1890 shoes are plentiful and fairly cheap. All men's and children's shoes are rarer than women's.

Hats. All women's hats and bonnets from the 1890s onwards are relatively plentiful, but those before that date may well be in a bad state or have had their trimmings removed. Any in a good condition will be expensive as hats are fairly delicate and, unless kept in a hat box, tend to get crushed easily and are often difficult to restore. Men's top hats and bowlers are quite common.

Gloves. The long white kid gloves used for evening wear survive in large numbers. They are difficult to date as styles changed little over a long period. Short kid gloves in white and other colours can be found but in fewer numbers. The really collectable gloves are the beautiful embroidered gauntleted gloves of the early seventeenth century which exist in reasonable quantities, but not surprisingly, are very expensive.

From the 1830s to 1860s black net mittens, sometimes finely embroidered, were very popular and these have survived quite well. Some interesting gloves were produced in the 1930s, usually French, and are attractive and unusual.

Fans. A very popular collecting field. There are a large number of fans in circulation, but the prices are now high for anything other than the fairly cheap late productions. Some people specialise in a particular type like those produced to advertise restaurants or hotels.

Bags. Although women did not regularly carry handbags until the beginning of this century there are various kinds around dating from the seventeenth century onwards. The earliest ones are small, usually embroidered, and fall into two kinds: flat ones for sweet herbs and round ones for money. You can still find eighteenth-century work-bags which are usually embroidered. During this period women carried their money and handkerchiefs in pockets tied round their waists and worn under their dresses. At the end of the century, with the introduction of flimsy dresses, they started to carry reticules which were often work-bags made to serve another purpose.

From the nineteenth century the commonest surviving item is

probably the netted money purse, sometimes decorated with steel beads. Other bags of this period are either of canvas work or embroidered satin, again, soft fabric bags more like the reticule than the type of handbag or purse used today.

Leather handbags made their appearance in the last quarter of the nineteenth century and were used for travelling rather than every-day bags. But more women were now working and needed stronger, more serviceable bags to hold money, keys, spectacles, diary, and all the other small items they needed to carry, even if the most conspicuous item of today's bag, the make-up case, was missing. The early bags tended to be stout and it is not really until the 1920s that pretty, decorative leather bags for the daytime became fashionable.

From this period too come many of the bead-embroidered bags, although this type was also prevalent from the early nineteenth century onwards. Bead bags are not easy to date unless the decoration obviously belongs to a particular period.

Flat textile accessories

These are the shawls, scarves and handkerchiefs, usually large, flat pieces of material, which are worn draped about the body in some way. The correct name for these items at any one time is confusing; for example, what was called a 'handkerchief' in the eighteenth century was a large square worn tucked into the neck of a dress. 'Shawl' and 'scarf' are equally confused.

Men's pocket handkerchiefs were often coloured with white spots and were usually a yard square. They are often called snuff handkerchiefs because the colour hid the brown-coloured mucus which came from the nose when snuff had been inhaled. Their size is comparable to a woman's large headscarf of today. Most ladies' pocket handkerchiefs which survive are the rather dainty lace-edged ones, sometimes with more lace than centre. Others are larger with embroidered corners or initials.

Then there is the printed commemorative handkerchief produced to mark some anniversary or event, like a coronation, jubilee or war. Most examples extant are nineteenth century in date but they were first produced in the eighteenth century.

Existing in fair numbers are the delicate whitework embroidered collars, sometimes very large and triple-tiered, which were popular in the 1820s and 1830s. They are known as 'pelerines' and were often of a very fine sheer cotton muslin. On some the decoration is

Ayrshire work with the intricate little filling stitches peculiar to that type of embroidery. However, they were produced all over the country by women called 'satin stitch workers'.

But perhaps the commonest and most impressive large, flat dress accessories are Paisley shawls. This term is used to cover all shawls which have the pine-cone motif, although they are not all woven or printed in Paisley. The largest were 11 ft by 5 ft 9 in. and known as plaids. Materials for these shawls vary but wool or wool and silk are the commonest. The early shawls, long and narrow with end borders only, are the ones found least often, while the plaid size with an all-over pattern or very deep end borders, dating to the 1850s and 1860s, is the most prevalent. They are also the variety collectors seem to prefer and are still bought by people to wear. Occasionally coats made in the present century from Paisleys turn up, and one Italian designer used them inside out to make men's suits in the 1960s.

Paisleys were based on the Kashmir shawl which also survives in some numbers. The difference is in the weaving, for Kashmirs are made by an elaborate and time-consuming twill-tapestry technique which makes them look like patchwork on the back. The Paisleys were woven on a draw-loom and later on a Jacquard loom, allowing very intricate patterns to be made. Whilst it is difficult to describe the appearance of these two techniques, once they have been seen side by side the difference is readily apparent.

As well as woven Paisleys there are a great variety of printed ones. These vary from those that are rather coarsely printed to others on beautiful, delicate wool and silk gauze.

In the twentieth century the embroidered silk shawl with fringe, available in bright colours or just one colour, was very popular. Called Chinese shawls, they are difficult to date because they were developed for the European market and are recorded as imports from the early nineteenth century. There is at least one painting of a woman wearing one of these shawls in about 1825, but the majority found today are probably from the 1920s. They were also reputed to be worked in countries other than China although the style remained the same.

6   A Jacquard woven Paisley shawl of plaid size, about 1860. This shows the full pattern which was never visible when the shawl was worn, as they were folded in half across the width. *Royal Scottish Museum, 1958.207*

Lace

This was avidly collected in the late nineteenth and early twentieth centuries but since the First World War it has fallen out of favour in Britain. In the last ten years, however, it has picked up as a popular collectors' field, although the prices have nowhere near reached the sums of eighty years ago. Many of the earlier collectors wore their laces for it was a very popular dress accessory at that period, but as they often altered them to suit their clothes it is now rare to find lace pieces in their original form. Lace cap lappets, for example, are often joined up to form a single necktie, or sleeve frills unpicked to form a bertha collar. This might not distress the lace collector but it can annoy the costume collector who wants to collect the pieces as dress accessories.

Today the interest in collecting hand-made lace goes with a

7   Lace fan and mittens. The fan leaf is of Brussels needle-made point de gazé, with gilded mother-of-pearl sticks and guards, dating from the late nineteenth century. The mittens are machine-made net with hand-made Honiton bobbin lace sprigs applied, dating from the second half of the nineteenth century. *Royal Scottish Museum, 1970.1090; 1971.116&A*

revived interest in making it, particularly bobbin lace. Before anyone begins to collect lace, however, the difference between hand-
made and machine-made laces should be learnt. Pat Earnshaw's
book, *The Identification of Lace* (Shire Publications, 1980), is very
useful in this respect. Nineteenth-century machine-made lace can
be very fine and technically extremely interesting, but it is the
hand-made laces which are the most sought after. Both varieties
made in the nineteenth and twentieth centuries abound. Earlier
laces are also fairly plentiful, but the spectacular pieces are expensive. There should be no difficulty in getting together a collection
representative of the types of laces produced, but it may be hard to
get really good pieces and they will be more costly. Larger pieces
made to shape such as shawls, veils and jackets will also be higher in
price.

Embroidery

This is plentiful but often pricey. If you have the money it is quite
possible to build up a good collection of British embroidery from the
late sixteenth century to the present, but the embroidered clothes of
the earlier period will be very hard to find.

Samplers, though not strictly speaking costume, have their own
specialist collectors and even the very common, and not very
attractive, late nineteenth-century alphabet samplers are not cheap
today. Seventeenth-century pieces are particularly expensive but
the market is unpredictable, as the recent sale of the Theodore H.
Kapnek Collection in America showed. It is not always the earliest
or most historic that will command the highest prices, but in Britain
and America thousands of pounds and dollars are paid for particularly desirable pieces.

Textiles

The most collected items here are the silks produced by the various
European centres until the end of the eighteenth century, and
include the beautiful early and mid-eighteenth-century silk brocades, many of which were woven at Spitalfields in London. These
heavy silks have lasted well and are still found in some numbers.
Last century many of the old dresses were re-used for things like
cushion covers or screens, so that there are more pieces of the dress
fabric available than there are dresses.

Printed furnishing cottons of the late eighteenth and early nineteenth centuries were fairly common in America, if not in Britain,

but in recent years the sources for these have dried up. Machine-printed textiles of the later nineteenth century are a neglected field. William Morris prints and the designer-produced fabrics of this century are now very much collectors' items, and correspondingly expensive.

The recent sharp price rise for pattern sample books, which are the records of textile firms' products, reflects the interest in them of modern designers. The Japanese, in particular, are buying up these books to reproduce them for the European and American markets, where the current interest in Victorian prints means it is cheaper to buy these old patterns than to design new ones. However, the results from modern silk-screen printing are less sharp than the original woodblock or roller prints and complicated patterns often have to be simplified. It is as well for the collector to be aware of these reproductions if she is interested in printed textiles.

Sample books are not easily stored and the main collectors tend to be people who have a use for them, or museums who collect them for their historic or technical value. Allied to sample books are the woodblocks, necessary for printing the fabrics, which sometimes turn up and have enjoyed a certain vogue as wall decorations. The lead plate and copper cylinders which were also used are not likely to be found as they were re-used or melted down for their scrap metal value; woodblocks were not re-usable in this way.

Quilts

A revival of interest in quilt-making both of the patchwork and blind-quilting varieties has created a great demand for old quilts. Already a popular collecting field in America, it is now catching on in Britain and auction houses are holding specialist sales. Most of those available derive from the late nineteenth or twentieth centuries but earlier ones occasionally appear.

Dolls' clothes

This is a specialist area within the doll-collecting field. Some dolls' clothes are very crudely made whilst others are perfect miniature reproductions of fashionable dress. They are found in doll sales and in shops specialising in dolls rather than with costume specialists.

Furs

It is rare to find anything of historic date in furs because they were so often remodelled. They are also extremely difficult to store well. The most usual items to find are muffs from the 1840s onwards and fur stoles and tippets. Coats are very rare.

Theatrical Dress

It is not always easy to distinguish theatrical from fancy dress. Before the present century most actors had to supply their own clothes for the theatre, and for historical settings often used original old clothes which they altered to suit the parts. This is one reason why so many eighteenth-century dresses are found altered. From the 1890s onwards many leading dressmakers made clothes especially for the 'modern dress comedies' of the day, and then sold similar designs to the public. Lily Elsie's 'Merry Widow' hat, which she wore in the stage musical, was very popular and set a fashion trend.

Costumes designed for well-known companies like Diaghilev's Ballets Russes, or by renowned painters and designers, are now extremely expensive.

EUROPEAN FOLK DRESS

The ethnic look has been a recurring fashion trend in recent years, causing the folk dress of both Europe and the rest of the world to be much sought after. As Britain does not have a folk dress tradition comparable to that found in the rest of Europe, there is little real understanding or interest in it on a research level, resulting in a disastrous lack of knowledge for the collector in this field.

Contrary to belief, folk dress did change in style over the years. It was influenced by fashionable dress and the technological advances which took place in the textile industries, as well as by local economic, social and political conditions. For this reason it is important to know when an outfit was made, but it is almost impossible to discover this information, because there are few books in English on the folk dress of other countries and those which do exist are usually too general to be of use. Folk dress studies vary widely from country to country and although the standard may be high in sociological or ethnographic content this is of little use to the costume collector who wants to identify pieces of costume.

Again, folk dress varies from village to village, from region to region, from season to season, from age to age and between the sexes. Some communities have incredibly elaborate costume codes, for example in one village in Czechoslovakia the women had a different cap for every Sunday in the year. It is therefore not enough to know that a particular item came from Czechoslovakia, you have to know the exact location.

Another problem is that most folk dress is made up of six or more items. The way they are worn and the combinations are indicative of the particular region, village, sex, age, occasion or social standing of the wearer. If the items are collected separately the chances of getting the right pieces to form an ensemble are remote. However, this is not to say that you should not collect these items but you must be aware of the difficulties.

Many people have collected folk dress in the past merely for the embroidery, while the rest of the garment was just thrown away. For instance, the white smocks worn as the basic undergarment in the Balkans frequently had their embroidered sleeve, neck and hem ends cut off.

There is a good deal of embroidery of this type still to be found which, although usually unprovenanced, can be attributed to a general area. It will be very unusual to find anything more than a hundred years old because folk dresses were worn every day and were renewed when they were worn out, so that it is only the garments worn most recently that survive or those set aside for special occasions such as weddings.

NON-EUROPEAN COSTUME

There are distinctive clothes for Court and aristocratic wear and a separate folk dress deriving from many of the cultures of the East. The Court dress is best known and survives in the largest numbers but, unlike its European counterpart, it changes relatively slowly in comparison to the seasonal variations of Paris, London or New York in the heyday of haute couture. This makes accurate dating to a precise year or decade impossible and irrelevant.

In many cultures the important thing is the style of dress worn by each grade within the Court system. The outstanding example is that of China where an elaborate code laid down what each level in the system should wear both in summer and in winter. As Chinese dress consists of several garments worn together to create a single ensemble, it is vital to ensure that the correct coat for a particular grade is worn with the correct trousers or skirt, and that summer

8 The costume of a seventh rank official, Chinese, nineteenth century. The official dragon robe, the *ch'i-fu*, is bright blue, with a dark blue silk coat, a *p'u-fu*, worn over it. This one is padded for autumn wear. The emblem of the seventh rank, a mandarin duck, is in silk tapestry weave panels, *k'o-ssu*, sewn to the front and back of the coat. A winter hat and black silk boots complete the outfit, whilst the trousers are concealed by the robes. *Royal Scottish Museum, 212.94; 1967.415&B, C; L.104.7B&E; 11L, 151*

and winter wear are not mixed up. Therefore, the problems facing the oriental collector are similar to those of the European folk dress enthusiast in assembling all the right garments.

The majority of Chinese costume came to the West in three main periods: the first was after the sacking of the Summer Palace in 1860; the second followed the Boxer Rebellion at the end of the century; whilst further pieces became available after 1924, when the remaining members of the Imperial family were finally made private citizens and the Court structure collapsed. Any really early clothing with a good provenance before the 1840s is extremely rare.

The availability of some types of oriental clothing is greater than others. Chinese is probably the most common, of which the beautiful embroidered and k'o-ssu (tapestry silk weave) coats are the most typical. They were great favourites for lounging, or as opera coats, in some fashionable circles in Europe during this century, so some may be found which have been subtly altered or taken in. There is also a fair number of women's pleated skirts.

Outside Japan it is rare to find any really spectacular examples of their marvellous textile tradition. The Japanese themselves have always valued their own culture very highly irrespective of the period and so the really beautiful kimonos have never been neglected. Today, although the Japanese collect Western art avidly, they are still just as enthusiastic about their own culture and consequently little of real worth comes out, or if it does it is at a price most collectors cannot afford. There is a dating problem with Japanese material but the majority of kimonos found in the salerooms, whilst being very attractive, are almost always less than a hundred years old.

Even more so than that in Europe, the folk and tribal dress of the Orient is usually of very recent date. Many tribes are nomadic and have no room for storing unneeded clothes. So, again, although there are changes in style over a period of time, it is very unlikely that much will be found surviving any earlier than the mid-twentieth century, except in museum collections.

Middle Eastern tribal dress has come into vogue in recent years with the increased interest in rugs and carpets. Among the most expensive pieces are the beautiful embroidered coats of the Türkmen tribes which inhabit an area now divided between the Soviet Union, north-east Iran and Afghanistan. These can still be found but are becoming rarer, and their modern counterparts are not as elaborately embroidered and are done on the sewing machine.

9 Costumes from the tribes of southern Iran. The woman's outfit is of the nomadic Qashqa'i from the south-west near Mehrigird, and was collected in 1974. It is made up from modern fabrics such as nylon, but constructed in a traditional style. The man on the right, from the same area, wears a block-printed cotton robe and the traditional felt hat. The man on the left is from the Bakhtiari of south Iran. These are everyday clothes. *Royal Scottish Museum, 1975.63, 64, 65&A, 61&A, 98, 99, 101*

India has always been rich in embroidery and textiles and there are several types of material from the subcontinent which turn up in fair numbers. There are large quantities of the printed cotton hangings known as palampores, many of which were brought back by Europeans who had lived in the East. Tray cloths, table cloths, cushions and other household wares were made in abundance by the Indians using their own traditional stitches and adapting their patterns for the Europeans who lived in India. These survive in very large numbers but most of this material is less than a hundred years old. Costume pieces are rarer.

One of the commonest Indian items in the salerooms is probably the Kashmir shawl. These are difficult to tell apart from the Paisleys because Paisley copied Kashmir, then Kashmir copied Paisley, but the technique is the main way of distinguishing between the two. The Kashmir is made up of mosaics of wool, each small piece woven in twill-tapestry weave, which means there are no continuous weft threads. There is often added embroidery at the bottom. Sales which include shawls usually have some of each kind and this is the best way of seeing the difference between the two techniques.

Embroideries from Turkey are quite common, the most usual being small towels – long, narrow pieces of white fabric worked at both ends. The embroidery usually consists of one motif which repeats about three times across the width and is quite distinctive in style.

Textiles have been preserved in the hot, dry sands of both Egypt and Peru. Both these cultures made very sophisticated textiles and excavations have brought a mass of material to light. Small fragments are often sold in the salerooms but larger pieces and complete garments are very rare.

Tribal groups, as soon as they came into contact with Europeans, often began to produce clothing adapted for them but based on authentic tribal wear. There are several well-known eighteenth-century portraits of men wearing adaptations of North American Indian dress. This old tourist material is rare and much sought after today. More readily available are pieces embroidered in beads and quill-work which were made in large quantities by various North American tribes. They range from octopus bags and mocassins to Glengarry-style hats and are quite often found in antique shops and sales and are relatively inexpensive.

A particular type of textile, the Navajo blanket, made by a North American tribe, has achieved a modern art form. These pieces are based on traditional designs and certain weavers' work is now very expensive.

Recently molas, a type of multi-layer appliqué patch found on women's blouses in the San Blas Islands, Panama, have become popular. These are still made and can be found in certain specialist shops. So too can costume pieces from other South and Central American countries.

In Africa traditional weaving survives in some areas, though modified by the use of factory-made yarns and synthetic dyes. Older pieces find their way into the salerooms on occasion and there are one or two specialist shops selling African textiles which sometimes have them.

In the Pacific bark cloth is still made in places but it is no longer used for clothing. It is produced either for ceremonial purposes – as wedding gifts, for example – or for tourist souvenirs. Old pieces are very rarely seen at sales.

Some dealers specialise in the beautiful textiles from Indonesia. These include both the batiks and ikats as well as woven fabrics. It is difficult to date many of these textiles but there were some very good batiks produced there in the 1930s. This material can also be found at sales.

FAKES

On the whole the costume and textile collector does not have to worry about fakes. There are certain antique Islamic textiles from the Buyid period which are now considered to be forgeries, but the average collector is unlikely to encounter these. Excavated textiles, which is what these Buyid fabrics are, lend themselves more to the faker's art than other varieties because they have suffered by being buried, thus making it easier to age them artificially.

The costume collector is going to find that the remodelling and alteration of clothes poses more of a problem. Remodelling can take place a year or so after the original making of a garment and is usually done to make it more up to date. Twenty or thirty years later the same process can happen again as a new generation becomes interested in or inherits older pieces. Fifty or a hundred years on it might be altered for fancy dress wear. This re-use of clothes is interesting in itself and a fascinating story can be pieced together from the various changes that have occurred.

When a dress is altered a long time after it was made the material may indicate at first sight that it is eighteenth century. However, the dress will have been altered to suit the fashions of the new period, for example the 1840s, and it will have the bodice shaping of that decade. Similarly even a fancy dress will show something of the style of fashionable dress of its period, no matter how carefully the antique original is followed.

Certain styles which make a return can cause some initial problems of dating, but as a rule an earlier design has been subtly altered to suit the modern taste and it can be easily spotted. Another problem with dresses from the 1920s onwards is that they may well be good copies made for the theatre or television. These are harder to recognise because recent trends have led to greater accuracy in the dressing of period drama. Although they are not made to deceive a costume collector, once they are sold from a drama wardrobe, they may well find their way onto the open market as originals.

FASHION PLATES AND PHOTOGRAPHS

These are two non-textile areas which are directly related to costume and therefore of interest to the collector.

Fashion plates are the coloured or monochrome engravings found in late eighteenth- and nineteenth-century magazines which were used to illustrate fashions before the invention of photography. They are sometimes very charming, especially when drawn by the better artists, but are often rather crude in the cheaper magazines. The plates usually started off from Paris and might be redrawn several times in the course of a year for magazines in London, Berlin or New York. Sometimes two or more figures would be amalgamated by the copier. How far these plates show actual dresses rather than the ideas of a dressmaker is not known. Certainly by the late nineteenth century Worth had many of his garments drawn for *The Queen* and *Harper's Bazar*.

Photography was invented in the 1830s and instantly became a great fad. In Britain David Hill and Robert Adamson were busy in Edinburgh taking portrait photographs between 1843 and 1846. Although the technique they used gives a slightly blurred effect, their surviving prints give a marvellous insight into the clothes of the professional class in a provincial city in the years covered. They also took some early photographs of occupational dress in the fishing town of Newhaven.

Later in the century the *carte de visite* became popular and provided a cheap portrait for a family to send out to relatives and friends scattered round the world. It became fashionable to collect photographs of royalty and famous people and stick them in albums. Many of these *cartes de visite* are not dated but some clues can be gleaned from the photographer's address on the back. Although

10 A photograph of Sir Henry and Lady Clavering of Axwell, taken by John Adamson, the brother of Robert. This shows the clothes of the 1850s with great clarity and is a good contrast to the fashion plates. *Royal Scottish Museum, Technology, 1942.1.1 p153*

they are posed these studio portraits do show how the clothes were worn, and are a useful corrective to the somewhat exaggerated drawings of the fashion plate.

Photography is now a major collecting field and prices are very high for top photographers' work. Fortunately the best ones for the costume collector are often of no interest to the photographic buff.

From what has been said so far it will be apparent that the costume which has survived today is only a minute fraction of what was produced in the past, and that it is not always representative of the whole range of material produced nor of all the different types of people who wore clothes or made textiles. The main thing to remember is the very nature of textiles and why everything is against the survival of this type of material. So why do some things survive and others do not?

In Europe it is rare for any clothes to survive before 1600, but there are exceptions. First, there are those buried in peat bogs, either by design or accident, where the acidity of the soil has stopped the bacterial decay of the fabrics, particularly wool. The oldest examples are those from the Bronze and Iron Age burials in Denmark. Very wet, waterlogged sites can sometimes have a similar effect and the recent spate of excavations in Britain on sites at Vindolanda, York, London and Perth have produced large quantities of textile fragments although there have so far been no major garment pieces. The fragments all came from rubbish tips in settlement areas so it would be unlikely that large garments would be found. These excavated sites date to the Roman, Anglo-Saxon, Viking and mediaeval periods.

In Greenland clothes from the bodies of settlers have been preserved in the frozen conditions and are most interesting because they belonged to ordinary people. The other end of the social scale has yielded clothes from the opened graves of princes and royalty from several European countries and also of bishops and priests. This type of find, though, is unevenly distributed and in some cases one type of fibre has been preserved whilst another has rotted, thus giving a distorted impression of the clothing worn. The amount that has been found is not large taken as a whole and whilst the clothes allow us to study the cut, the fabric scraps from excavations often tell us more about the trade and economy of a country, because they represent a wider cross-section of fabrics used.

In Europe the veneration of saints' relics has led to the survival of some interesting early silks. These objects of piety, usually small pieces of bone, were wrapped in fragments of silk which was often imported from the East and obviously very expensive and precious in its day. A certain number of saints' clothes have also survived.

Another reason for survival is sentiment. In Sweden three members of the aristocratic Sture family became martyrs when they were murdered by an unpopular king in the late sixteenth century. The clothes they wore when they were killed were preserved in Upsala Cathedral and displayed for many years as a reminder of the king's tyranny, and they have lasted to the present day.

The main survivals from the period before 1600 are ecclesiastical garments such as copes and chasubles. These were usually of very expensive silks and velvets richly embroidered and presented to the church by kings and wealthy members of the community. Because of the quantity that a wealthy church, monastery or cathedral acquired during the centuries there was less wear on the individual items. When the ritual changed the vestments were usually remodelled so that some existing pieces are made of earlier fabric. As the silk brocades and velvets were inherently stronger than the thinner silks and taffetas they have survived quite well.

More of these vestments survived on the Continent than in Britain despite the almost constant warfare in Europe in the sixteenth and seventeenth centuries in the wake of religious upheavals. Scotland, in particular, suffered badly and there is only one example of non-secular embroidery which can be dated to before the Reformation and that is an unfinished piece known as the Fetternear Banner.

During the last century many religious houses on the Continent were closed down for various reasons and their vestments sold. They became the source of the main collections of mediaeval silks in museums today. The robes were usually cut up into small pieces and sold to separate institutions which explains why the same design can be seen in museums in Britain, the Continent and America. The likelihood of any more mediaeval silks in such quantity coming onto the market again is now remote.

The last quarter of the sixteenth century in England saw an outburst of domestic embroidery. Every piece of clothing that could be decorated was covered in black work or multi-coloured silks, often in flower or animal designs. The paintings of the period reveal a very rich tradition which flowered for about sixty years from the 1560s to the 1620s. It would seem that an enormous amount of embroidery must have been produced and a reasonable amount survives. Today we see it as both charming and naïve but it was very skilfully worked by both amateur and professional needlewomen. Apart from one or two isolated examples, such as James I & VI's suit (now in a private collection), complete outfits do not survive, but there are a number of jackets for men and women, gloves, coifs and smocks all richly embellished and treasured by later generations for their embroidery. Some pieces were cut up when they became unfashionable and made into useful household items thereby ensuring their survival.

Whilst the needlework of the mid-seventeenth century, particularly the raised-work boxes and pictures, has survived in quantity, the plain silk dresses have all been re-used. The earliest woman's dress remaining in Britain is one in silver tissue from the 1660s now in the Museum of Costume at Bath, followed by a mantua of about 1709 to be found at Shrewsbury. These are exceptional, however, because neither men's nor women's garments survive as complete sets in any number until the 1740s. Surprisingly, perhaps, there are more men's clothes from the seventeenth century than women's and there are enough to show the main development throughout the period.

Accessories are a different matter and shoes, gloves and bags survive in fair numbers. But underwear, usually being of plain linen, has long gone except for the odd item belonging to a well-known historical figure like the Duke of Monmouth.

Why is this pattern of survival so marked? One reason is that until the mid-eighteenth century clothes were an expensive commodity and were regularly left in wills to relatives and friends. Despite fashion changes very few people would consider buying clothes at the rate that we do today, even in wealthy circles. Cloth was very expensive and in an age of profligate living, such as the early seventeenth century, an extremely wealthy man like Robert Cecil, Earl of Salisbury, could die heavily in debt because of the style of living considered necessary to his position. Several nobles were virtual bankrupts and their estates never recovered from the extravagance of these years. We know from their portraits that much of their money was lavished on their clothes, but apart from a few shoes and gloves and other odds and ends the rest has gone.

The perquisites of office in the period before the Victorians made many inroads on clothes too. Maids and valets considered it their right to have the clothes of their employers. Sometimes they were given after only one wearing, sometimes after a season, and an employer who did not pass on clothes might find difficulty in getting a good maid or valet. The employees might not wear the clothes themselves but would sell them in the thriving second-hand market. Lesser nobles, or younger sons out to cut a dash on no income, might well buy the showy items, but a good plain satin suit with the more frivolous trimmings removed would have been useful to a much wider group of men. A warm cloak or a hat would be serviceable too, but the courtier's thin shoes would be of no use to the countryman.

Clothes were cut up for children and those who were thrifty would remodel items that were left to them or handed on from richer relatives. The plain silks of the seventeenth century were obvious candidates for remodelling or for using for anything needing plain material. In the days before dry cleaning silk did not have the kind of life that we now expect and the plainer the colour the more likely the stains were to show. So the pressures on the clothes were intense and the survival of particular groups of items is therefore the exception rather than the rule.

In the middle of the eighteenth century fashionable wide side-hoops displayed the heavily patterned brocades and damasks which were the glory of the French and British silk industries. There were seasonal variations each year in fabric patterns but changes in dress design were much slower. These hoops were worn in their most exaggerated form at Court for a royal Drawing Room or Birthday, and a new dress had to be worn on each occasion. The wearer, therefore, either had to alter the dress to a style more suitable for everyday wear or else get rid of it by gift or sale. Thus Court mantuas are rather rare in their original state although some have undoubtedly survived because their heavy embroidery made them impossible to alter to a simpler style. The material of these dresses has survived well even if the garments have suffered alteration at the hands of dressmakers over the last two hundred years.

Eighteenth-century portraits show the majority of their subjects wearing plain silk or satin dresses, but these plain silks are rarer survivors and suffered the same fate as those in the previous century. With so many patterned silks surviving it is curious that artists should have shown so few. They may have felt that plain colours were easier to paint and more flattering to the sitter since the face would stand out rather than the dress.

11   Court mantua and petticoat, about 1760. The silk is either English or French, dating to about 1752–65. This large blue and white pattern shows to advantage on the wide side hoops which were obligatory for Court wear. The front of this mantua is shown in photo 35. *Royal Scottish Museum, 1977.241&A*

Printed cotton and linen dresses were worn by all classes in the eighteenth century but have lasted less well than silk ones. They were much more likely to be passed on to maids and worn by them, and as they could be easily washed they had a much longer, more useful life than patterned silks.

In the eighteenth century the economic and social changes taking place help to explain why a greater number of garments have survived. Clothes ceased to be left in wills, perhaps a good indication that they were becoming more generally available and cheaper. The great technical achievements in the cotton industry at the end of the century led to increased production and a fall in prices. New roads and transport systems opened up the country, making visiting and the social round in London – the Season – practical. This meant that the importance of clothes changed in emphasis and a wider group of people could afford to follow fashion.

When clothes became cheaper the leaders of society bought more to underline their position, and so fashions began to change more quickly. Stylish outfits were introduced for different times of the day and for special activities such as archery or the opera. It is sometimes difficult for us to distinguish between a dinner dress, a ball gown and an opera outfit but a woman of the period would have known.

There was a population explosion in the early nineteenth century which continued throughout the period, meaning that there were more people to be clothed, and as extra clothes were produced their chances of survival increased. Larger families had houses big enough to hold all the clothes the family needed and when out of fashion the garments could be stored in attics, often remaining there until the last member died and the house was cleared out.

Although the second-hand clothes trade was just as flourishing in the nineteenth century as it had been previously, certain things were probably disposed of more frequently than others. For example good cloth suits and warm winter dresses in plain fabrics were more suitable for passing down the social scale than ball dresses or elaborate silk ones. However, moths eat garments made of wool and the chances of these surviving, despite the larger numbers made, were greatly reduced.

Children's clothes were handed down even in wealthy families and so wore out but baby clothes, which were made in large quantities, still exist in abundance. No Victorian woman could be certain that she would not be having another baby and some were probably kept 'just in case'.

Trimmings, buttons and lace were removed carefully in thrifty households and put away, and when a dress needed retrimming then the 'bit box' would be searched. This policy of thrift was common in many households before the present time.

Oddities of survival occur for other reasons. Dresses made for women who were particularly small, like Queen Victoria, are more likely to last than those made for the average woman, as they would not contain enough material to allow them to be remodelled for a larger woman. Similarly, dresses for women with physical peculiarities, such as a very long, narrow torso, might survive because they were not easy to adapt. There are also many dresses made for large, wide women which perhaps defeated the dressmaker by proving too much of a task for alteration.

The answer to the question about the size of our ancestors cannot be judged accurately by the surviving garments because the record is uneven. There are physical differences due to better diet and better medical care between the past and present generations, but in the recent past they were not a race of near dwarfs as some people seem to think. Because each dress was made to fit a particular person there is more room for variation in old clothes than in more recent ones, which are nearly all made to a standard set of sizes and consequently fit less well. A large group of people seen today vary in height, in bone structure and in the relationship of the parts of the body to each other; the people of the past were equally varied.

Clothes were put away for sentimental reasons such as the death of a beloved only child or the death of a husband, which meant that his widow had to put away her coloured dresses. This is a rarer phenomenon today but in the nineteenth century the wearing of mourning dress for prolonged periods was usual.

We keep far fewer clothes today than the people of the nineteenth or early twentieth centuries did. Second-hand clothes shops of all grades will buy fashionable, nearly new clothes, and thrift shops and jumble sales are all well attended by people who could afford to buy new. What are kept are usually items of great personal significance – wedding dresses, first dance dresses, a dress that the wearer felt particularly good in, or the very expensive dress bought for a special occasion and never suitable for any other. But we keep them for shorter periods as people move more frequently these days.

It would be interesting to know if the Queen has enough room to keep all the magnificent dresses Norman Hartnell made for her and which have contributed so much to her image. Perhaps they too have found their way into other hands as the clothes of her ancestors did. Even coronation robes were officially perquisites of various officers of state until Queen Victoria decided to keep all her robes and vestments. The only surviving coronation robes before Victoria are one or two pieces belonging to George IV and Queen Adelaide's velvet train. In some countries, such as Russia, the sovereign's garments were considered state property, and so the wedding and coronation garments of all the Czars exist from the eighteenth century onwards.

Otherwise, even the most personal items of royal clothing were regarded as perquisites of office. It is difficult to believe, however, that all the underwear which survives with Queen Victoria's monogram on it belonged to her. Although she would have had regular sets made at least once every two or three years they were of good quality linen which could have been passed on.

There is a story told of how Queen Victoria and Prince Albert, walking down Windsor High Street, saw two of the Queen's dresses hanging up outside a second-hand clothes shop. They were labelled as the Queen's and were looking very grubby. Both the Queen and the Prince were horrified as it offended their dignity to see her former clothes for sale in such a dirty state. After that all garments from members of the Royal Family had to be disposed of anonymously.

CHAPTER THREE

Building your collection

AUCTIONS

As a separate subject costume began to interest the auction houses in the late 1960s. The first regular specialist sales of costume were held by Christies in 1967, although there are records of sales of large private collections earlier in the century. Phillips and now Sotheby's have started regular sales in London, while Christies continue at their South Kensington branch with almost weekly sales. Other auction houses such as Bonhams and Harrods have also held specialist costume and textile sales, and this type of material is often included in the out-of-London salerooms of the three major houses as well as by provincial houses.

Auctions are not recommended for the novice collector to attempt straight away, but they are a good way of learning about the type of clothes still available. Usually you can view a day or two before the actual sale and a catalogue, sometimes illustrated, is produced which lists the items and gives a brief description. The accuracy of the identification and dating of any object depends on the expertise of the cataloguer. There is much more room for individual inter-pretation in costume and textile dating and identification than in many other types of object which find their way into the saleroom, so viewing is absolutely essential before you buy.

It is also a good way of learning about clothes because you can study details of cut, sewing and design. The collector can pit her judgment on date against the cataloguer's and can find out what the item is estimated to fetch. It really is a good idea to attend at least one sale, before starting to bid yourself, to see how it is done. Each saleroom varies slightly in the way its sales are arranged but basically the methods are the same.

The auctioneer normally sits at a desk facing the audience with a copy of the catalogue which he annotates as the sale proceeds. He often has an assistant to help write down the names of the buyers and the prices realised. As each lot is called by the auctioneer yet another assistant holds it up so that the audience can check it before starting to bid. Mistakes sometimes occur when lots get muddled, so be sure that what is being sold fits the description.

The auctioneer will open the bidding at about or below the lowest estimated price, and if no one responds he will drop the price until someone starts to bid. The bidding continues until only one person is left, but it is rarely so quick that a collector would miss a chance if she wanted to bid. To attract the auctioneer's attention merely raise your catalogue or hand to a level where it can be seen.

Another thing to remember is that bids are usually in a set number of pounds per bid. For items of low value it may go up £3, £5, £8, £10, and then by £5 or £10 leaps and so on. It depends on the interest in the item and the auctioneer's judgment of the quickness of each bidder's response as they up the price. It is a mistake to call out things like, 'I bid £15', when the next step would normally be £10, and bidders should not wave their catalogues around to up the bid when it is already with them.

The saleroom makes the adrenalin flow quicker and it is very easy to bid higher than you can afford. This is unwise and will be regretted afterwards, so be sensible and make a very firm rule never to go higher than a set upper limit. Mark the catalogue accordingly, even if you use a code, for each lot number in which you are interested, and then stick to it. Bear in mind that in some British salerooms there is a 10 per cent buyer's premium with 15 per cent VAT on top of that. Of course, if unsuccessful on an earlier lot you may have a little more for a later one, but on the whole do not be tempted. Auctions are unpredictable affairs and it only needs one rich and determined collector, or a dealer who has *carte blanche* for a client, for the prices to become ridiculously high. Another time bad weather or illness might keep the prices low because the competition just is not there.

One or two further points about auctions are worth mentioning. Many items may well have a reserve price on them and if this is not reached then they are not sold. Of course, this reserve is not made public and these lots are described as 'bought in'. The items may well be entered at a later sale when the reserve will have been removed and they will be sold for whatever they can raise.

Bids can be left at the auction house if collectors cannot go to the sale themselves and either the auctioneer or an assistant will do the bidding on their behalf. It is not always obvious when this happens but the auctioneer might say, 'The bid is with me', meaning that he has a bid left by an absentee which is higher than those offered in the room. If no one raises the bid then the item is sold to the absentee buyer.

It is usually possible to pay for and collect items immediately after the sale, although arrangements for this will vary and new customers will probably have to pay cash. It is as well to check up on this beforehand and to be prepared. Storage charges are usually added if the goods are not collected after about two days. Do not forget about the buyer's premium and VAT, and sellers pay a charge at all houses.

In America auctions which include costume are held by all the main houses. Sometimes there are separate sales; sometimes it is included in sales of related topics. Auctions are often conducted at a slightly brisker pace than in Britain and the would-be bidder needs to be alert. There is also a slightly different bidding system in some houses where buyers register their names before the sale and are handed a piece of wood with a number painted on it. When bidding, this 'paddle' is used and the number of the successful bidder noted. This means that the whole process is anonymous.

In all cases the conditions relating to buyers at auctions should be studied carefully. These are normally printed in the front of each catalogue or at smaller auction rooms are available for consultation at the viewing.

SHOPS, SALES, FAIRS

Apart from auctions there are a great variety of other places where you can find old clothes and textiles for sale. There are few antique shops which sell just clothes, but several specialise in selling old clothes for wearing and they might well keep some garments which are difficult to sell for this purpose but are suitable for the collector. This is probably more common outside London where there is enough trade in both fields for shops to specialise.

In addition there is the genuine second-hand shop selling more recent wearable goods. Here you can find modern couture garments, though at a much higher price than would be paid at a jumble sale or a thrift shop, for everything is still fashionable and stock is strictly limited to the current season's wear.

Then there are the thrift shops, often run by some charity such as Oxfam on a semi-permanent basis. These sometimes hold specialist sales when their more antique stock of clothes – those which are not in current fashionable taste – are sold as collectors' items. The goods are usually priced by an auctioneer or valuer so will tend to be more expensive than at a jumble sale, but as the charity will want a quick sale it will certainly be cheaper than an antique shop.

Jumble sales can be a good source for finding garments, but the type and quality of the items depends on the area and the organisation running the sale. This is possibly the cheapest source of all.

12   Gloves and stockings for a woman. Beige leather gloves with large gauntlets popular in the 1930s. The lisle thread stockings were worn until the mid-1950s when nylon stockings became cheap enough for everyday wear. These still have the maker's label and markings. *Royal Scottish Museum, 1963.381&A; 1975.236&A*

A recent trend in Britain has been the growing number of antiques fairs and bazaars. Some of these offer good material, others are rather indifferent, but on the whole they are not particularly good for finding costume. However, if you collect accessories the fairs are places where shawls, bags, fans and parasols, not to mention photographs, may be found, so for some they are worth attending. Antique collectors' magazines are helpful in planning which fairs to attend as they list them in advance.

Art and Antiques is a weekly news magazine for collectors and has a full fairs' calendar for the coming week covering the whole country, as well as a list of forthcoming auctions. There are short articles on different types of collectors' material, a look at some exhibitions, book reviews and news items on topics of interest to collectors.

The Antique Dealer and Collectors Guide is a monthly magazine with a list of the main fairs for the coming month, a look at saleroom prices for the past month and articles on a very varied category of collectors' items.

Other useful aids are the *Guide to the Antique Shops of Britain* and the *Guide to the Antique Shops of London*, which are published by the Antique Collectors Club. These list the various shops and give an idea of their main interests. As these guides are published each year the information is kept up to date. There are a vast number of antique shops in Britain, and for the costume or textile specialist it is useful to be able to do some weeding out. However, this should not stop the collector from always looking in any likely shops 'just in case'. The collector of things like shawls, bead bags, fans or parasols can often find the odd item in a more general antique shop.

In North America there are a number of charity shops which sell antique clothes, such as The Lighthouse, Spence Chapin and Goodwill Industries, and they sometimes hold special sales. On a different level there are garage or tag sales, or swop meets, where home-owners get rid of their unwanted rubbish to anyone who wants to buy it. These are usually held at weekends and can be less than rewarding, but it does depend on the collector's interests. As in Britain the main antiques magazines list the shops and main fairs or shows. These include *Antiques*, which is a monthly, and although it rarely has articles on costume it does list the shows and has had several textile articles. In Canada *Ontario Showcase* lists the antique shops of the area once a year, and magazines such as *Canadian Antiques* and *Canadian Collector* list shops and shows.

GIFTS

Another source for the collector is the private gift or sale. Many people, when clearing out a house after the death of a relative, are quite glad to find someone interested in taking the old clothes which are not suitable for giving to a charity. This may mean that in order to have something she really wants the collector has to take items of no interest to her. In this case do not offer more than you are prepared to pay for the things you want, unless you can sell off any of the other pieces. But be fair and tell the seller this. When buying from private people do offer a good price because they are bound to hear sooner or later that someone else has sold the same thing for a larger sum. If people are really intent on making money then they will probably take their items to a shop or an auction house, so if they are prepared to sell to an individual collector it usually means they are not looking for the highest price. Nevertheless, if you value your reputation as a collector always offer a realistic amount.

In the past a gift of costume would not have been considered a thing of any monetary worth. Now, with prices for everything going up and up, costume has become another collecting field. A collector must use her own judgment, especially when offered something by someone she does not now but which she recognises to be valuable. Old people are often rather embarrassed to take money for old clothes unless they know it is very much older than they are. If it has some sentimental value, such as a mother's wedding dress, it could be tactless to offer money when all they want is a good home for it.

This leads to another delicate point, especially with regard to older people. When a gift is accepted it is as well to ensure that the donor knows what the collector intends to do with it. It might be rather upsetting for someone to discover that their mother's trousseau underwear will be used publicly at a fashion show when they had thought it would just be added to a private collection. Strictly speaking, once a gift has been made the original owner has no rights over the items, but it might cause bad feeling if collectors are not scrupulous in their dealings with private people. It is usual in museums for donors who request anonymity to have this wish respected, although the information may well be kept in files. If a private collector is asked to keep a gift anonymous then she should do so.

IMPORT AND EXPORT

Those who buy in a foreign country, either at auction or in shops, should study the export restrictions of those countries and the import conditions of their own country. In America, for example, it is illegal to import anything made of certain protected animal species unless there is a certificate to say that the piece is an antique. In Britain it is illegal to export antique items over a certain value without a licence. Nearly all countries now have complex laws on the import and export of antiques and a collector can be very heavily fined, as well as having all goods confiscated, for breach of the rules.

CHAPTER FOUR

Storage and handling

Although costume is not an asset which increases in value as quickly as a painting, it can deteriorate fast if not stored properly and handled with care, so knowing how to handle old textiles is vital.

HANDLING

It is very tempting to finger and stroke fabrics, and people do so continuously in clothes shops. Whilst an adult's hands are unlikely to be as dirty as a child's, the hands are one of the main areas for perspiration in the body and the acidity of sweat, not to mention any dust which sticks to the moisture, can cause problems. Old textiles should not be handled any more than is strictly necessary. Hands should be clean and dry before the pieces are touched and anyone with very sweaty hands should use their finger tips rather than their whole hand, or wear clean white cotton gloves.

When picking up a garment do not hold it too long by a delicate point. Heavy bead-embroidered dresses, such as those of the 1920s, must be well supported, and if possible looked at flat on a table. The base material of these dresses is often very fragile and the weight of the beads, which can be several pounds, can tear the fabric all too easily. The beads were sewn on by machine using a chain stitch and if a thread is cut then the stitches start unravelling and the beads fall off. It is not easy to repair these dresses, especially if the material is weak, so treat this type of dress with care all the time.

Clothes in the past were made to fit particular people and if someone tries on a dress today and does not have the same body shape, or is not wearing the right foundation garment, then it will probably not fit very well. If garments are too small anywhere, even by an inch, the seams could be strained, causing them to split. When trying old clothes on do be very careful about make-up and lipstick as these are some of the most difficult stains to remove, even from modern clothes.

Viewing at a sale can be a particular hazard because several dozen people will come in and look, whereas only a handful may actually attend the sale. It is part of the tourist scene in London to go to the salerooms and often the tourist has no interest in, or idea about, how to handle the articles shown. Careless handling by so many people means that garments in a frail condition can deteriorate before the sale is held.

STORAGE

Unlike a collection of porcelain, paintings, glass or silver, costumes have to be stored rather than displayed. Most collectors owning pieces which are not subject to light degradation can display their collection all over the house, and have enjoyment from it every day. Textiles are a different matter. One sampler collector has solved the problem by framing his collection and putting a little curtain over each one, so that they are mostly protected from the light unless he wants to show them. This is suitable for flat pieces which can be framed but is not practicable for the majority of costume.

Once you begin collecting it is easy to end up with several hundred pieces in a few years, so it pays to work out a good system to start with. There are two schools of thought which advocate 'hanging' or 'non-hanging' ways of storage. Non-hanging, that is laying the garments flat in drawers, is generally regarded to be the safest method, but is often the least practical for both the public and the private collector.

Non-hanging storage
As fabrics suffer when they are subjected to strain it is logical that hanging them up is not the best way of storing them, because the entire weight of the garment is dependent on the strength of the shoulders or waist. But as folding can add creases, which can lead to permanent marks and eventually to the splitting of the material, it follows that even laying garments flat has its problems. Ideally the drawers for clothes should be long enough to take the full length of the garments without folding, and wide enough to take a skirt's

width. There should be no more than one garment per drawer, and all folds should be padded with tissue paper to prevent sharp creases forming. This is the ideal, but in practice there has to be some modification.

The system devised in the Royal Scottish Museum was to have drawers of a size which could be manageable without being too cumbersome to transport inside the store. The area available was limited and fairly cramped due to air-conditioning ducts and the cellar height. The drawers were made to a uniform size of 2 ft 6 in. wide × 5 ft long × 6 in. deep. It was not possible to have two depths of drawer so a compromise size was chosen. They are made of a plastic material which looks like fibreboard. The base is plywood on the outside and the sides are held out by a strong, rigid metal frame round the top with plastic folded over it and studded. There are two carrying handles along each long side. The plywood base of the drawer slides on wooden fillets in the cupboard. If space had been available it would have made handling much easier if the drawers could have been pulled out on fillets on the inside of the doors so that their weight would have been well supported when they were drawn out.

Because of the depth of the drawers and the size of the collection it is not possible to put only one garment in each, so they are placed one on top of the other. Certain items, such as an early seventeenth-century leather fencing doublet, are padded to shape and put in a drawer on their own because they are delicate. Heavy brocade dresses of the eighteenth century take up a lot of room when they are folded and padded so only two or three will fit in, whereas too many muslin ones can be crammed into the drawers if care is not taken.

Two categories do not fit into these drawers at all well. These are ecclesiastical vestments and the heavily beaded dresses of the 1920s which, ideally, should be put into much shallower drawers. Architects' plan chests or map cabinets are quite good for these as the drawers are very shallow.

The drawers and cupboards were made for the Museum to particular specifications and were fairly expensive. However, as museum collections are expected to last, if not until the end of time at least for several generations, curators have to think in terms of hundreds of years, so expense is relative.

Many museums still have to store their collections in boxes and for the private collector this is probably the most practical solution for flat storage. If you have a sizeable collection it is easier to get boxes made to the required size and order yourself a large enough quantity. The initial outlay may be expensive but you will have better boxes which will last longer.

The Royal Scottish Museum has some boxes which were devised by the conservator for temporary storage. They are 23 in. × 15 in. × 5 in. and made of a strong cardboard which is bonded on the inside to a thin polythene coating. There is a hinged lid which is attached by brass staples to prevent rust, and on the short ends there are ventilation holes covered by acid-free paper. The holes allow the air to circulate while the paper prevents dirt and insects getting in. The boxes are strong enough to be stacked and to take heavy items.

There are ways of obtaining boxes free. Flower shops are a good source and their boxes are long, if not particularly wide. They may be fairly collapsible, needing struts in the corners to keep them firm, and the large ventilation holes should be covered. These are usually robust boxes because flowers are delicate.

Dress boxes are a thing of the past but some shops might still have them for wedding dresses, or other elaborate gowns. Shoe shops are another source; even if their boxes are not quite large enough to take a pair of old shoes comfortably they are very useful for gloves, small bags and other accessories. It is worth looking at what kinds of boxes local traders have thrown out with the rubbish and then you can ask them for similar ones. Carpet firms, for example, have rollers which can be used for storing large, flat textiles.

Once you have the boxes they must be made acceptable for storing costume. Because the making of paper and cardboard involves a high proportion of acid, which remains in the products, the boxes will have to be lined. All tissue paper used next to textiles should be acid free. This can be bought in small packets from all good stationers, but for the quantity a collector needs it should be bought by the ream, which a large stationer can order for you.

Tissue paper in contact with non-acid-free card should be changed fairly frequently as some of the acid will leach out onto the tissue. A further measure is to line the box with aluminium kitchen foil, while the polythene-lined boxes are inert so no special lining is needed for them.

For lining drawers in the Museum an unbleached calico is used, and although the plastic the drawers are made of is said to be inert it was decided to line them as an extra precaution. These linings are merely a length of calico which is twice as long as the drawer, plus a foot or so to overlap, and it just wraps round the contents. Between each garment and the next a layer of unbleached gauze is laid, making it easier to lift garments out of the drawers by taking hold of the gauze at both ends. The slightly rough surface of this material means that the clothes stick to it and do not move, so very little rearranging is necessary when they go back into the drawer.

Calico and gauze must be unbleached because in the bleaching of cotton cloth a strong chemical is used and not all of it is removed when the cloth is finished. The material should be washed first to remove any dressing and to shrink it before use. As it is used in great quantity the Museum buys it by the piece, but it is not difficult to obtain in most large cities and you can buy it in any quantity.

Another storage method, if cupboards are available, is based on the polythene trays that bakers use for carrying bread and cakes. These are strong and light in weight and come in a variety of sizes and depths suitable for a number of different objects. The trays are available from suppliers to the trade and come in different colours, with solid or pierced bases, and can be stacked. They would suit

13 One of a variety of moulded trays used by bakers and suitable for storing costume accessories. Inside it is a lightly padded wooden coat-hanger with a loose calico cover. The hat is a child's cloche in straw of the 1920s, and the shoes date to about 1910. Both the hat and the shoes have been well padded with acid-free tissue paper to help them keep their shape. *Royal Scottish Museum, 1974.175; 1966.265&A*

hats and shoes particularly well but could also be used for many types of accessory.

The arrangement of boxes or drawers is important. Museums spend a lot of time on keeping location lists up to date so that the exact whereabouts of each object is known. This is vital when a collection is very large and when the personnel in charge of it change at intervals. It is also necessary because auditors do spot checks every year on a random selection of numbers taken from the registers. For the private collector such an elaborate system will be unnecessary, but, the more a collection grows the less easy it is to remember each item in detail.

Similar items can go in each drawer or box. Cupboards of drawers mean that dresses, for example, can be stored in order of date, or with day and evening dresses separated. Coats might be in another cupboard, underwear in another, and heavy clothes separated from lightweight ones so that the latter are not crushed. A list of the contents of each drawer inside the cupboard door is a good idea so that the contents of each can be seen at a glance.

Racking is needed for the storage of boxes and wooden shelving can be made to fit if they are all the same size. It is a mistake to have too many on each shelf, and two is ideal. Sticky labels, which can be easily changed if necessary, are the best way to note the contents of each box. Labels should be put on the side which faces outwards so that they can be read without having to pull the boxes out.

Adjustable metal shelving, such as Dexion, is also suitable but might be rather expensive. However, there are often office or factory sales where you can pick up all kinds of potentially useful pieces which can be adapted to suit your needs. Filing cabinets, old birds' egg and insect cupboards can all be useful. When considering old cabinets remember that the costume will have to be protected from the acids in wood and from sharp metal edges. Oak is a very acidic wood and if possible should be avoided.

Hanging storage
In a museum where the staff are expected to get out items for visitors to see, it is practical for them to have some garments hanging up in wardrobes. They have to balance the wear and tear of getting the garments out of drawers against any strain from hanging in cupboards. In the Royal Scottish Museum a compromise was reached by having a representative selection of garments hanging in cup-

boards. Only those items which were strong enough to hang, and were not too heavy, were chosen.

The Museum's hanging cupboards are deeper than a normal wardrobe, being 2 ft 6 in. The height was determined by the ceiling of the cellar, which is domed, but at 5 ft 7 in. to the hanging rail it is, in fact, the best height for the average woman to reach comfortably. The hanging rail is a very strong one set 3 in. from the roof of the cupboard so that the hanger can go over the rail easily. The strength of the rail is important because costume is heavy and an ordinary wardrobe rail tends to sag in the middle from the weight. On the outside, above the cupboard doors, there is another hanging rail so that the dresses can be hung up for viewing. It is very wearing on the arms to hold up a long dress, even for a few minutes, to stop its hem from trailing on the floor, and this rail has been one of the most appreciated points in the cupboards' design.

All the cupboards have dust seals of velvet ribbon on the doors, while the hanging cupboards also have calico on the bottom so that trains and long skirts trail on a clean cloth which can be laundered when it gets dusty, for although the store is air-conditioned it is not completely dust free. If a storeroom is very dusty it may be necessary to make a complete calico dust-cover for the inside of the hanging cupboards.

For hanging costumes you need coat-hangers, but there are very few on the market which are perfect. The wire ones and the moulded plastic ones should both be avoided. Wire hangers are dangerous on two grounds; they can lose their coating and then rust, causing damage to the costumes, and they are difficult to pad sufficiently to stop hard creases forming on the shoulders. The moulded plastic variety, especially those for suits with a trouser rail, are moulded to the shape of modern posture with rounded shoulders. The rail tends to poke out in the back of clothes and the shoulder is too wide for many older garments.

Because the shoulders of women's dresses of the past may well be less broad than modern ones, the best coat-hangers to use are wooden since these can be cut down to fit the shoulders exactly. All hangers should be padded, not only to support the dresses better and prevent any hard shoulder-line creases, but also to protect the garments from any splinters, rust or acid leach from wood or metal. The best materials to use are unbleached calico and grey skin wadding, or one of a terylene variety. If the trouser rail is not required then a square of wadding can be cut and wrapped over the hanger's triangular shape. If the rail is needed then strips of wadding will have to be wound round each side. Even for just hanging up a skirt it is a good idea to put something like gauze on the rail so that the loops on the skirt have something to grip. A loose calico cover to slip over the padding is necessary to stop wadding fluff getting onto the clothes and can be taken off and washed occasionally. If preferred, the calico can be tacked loosely over the padding to keep it from slipping. Whichever method is chosen it should be the easiest and cheapest to suit the collection.

Use enough padding on the hangers to make the shoulder-line soft and rounded, but not so much that it distorts the line and puts another strain on the garment. Skirts should be hung up by four pairs of tapes if possible so that any strain is evenly distributed. Bias-cut dresses of the 1930s are best stored flat. So too are heavily bead-embroidered dresses of any period. Many of the very elaborately draped skirts of the 1880s will also need to lie flat because the strain on the waistband will be far too great for hanging. Trousers and breeches for both men and women are much better lying flat full length, but if they must hang it is better to put them over the well-padded rail of a hanger than to store them suspended from the waistband or leg ends by a grip-hanger. The coats of men's suits, especially modern ones, can be hung up, but some women's coats and jackets without fastenings will be much better flat. It helps to keep the shape of a coat if the fastenings are done up and padding is put in to hold out the chest where the shoulders or front are already heavily padded. If space is available men's coats should always be well padded before they are stored flat.

Rolled storage

Large textiles, such as Paisley shawls, quilts or bedspreads, should be stored rolled. Cardboard rollers used for carpets are quite suitable for this. They should be covered first in aluminium kitchen foil and then in tissue paper. The pieces to be rolled should be laid out face downwards on a flat surface which is slightly rough and tissue paper should be laid over the piece. Then roll it fairly tightly with more tissue paper between each layer so that there are no creases in it. A length of calico can be wrapped round the outside to protect the item from light and if it is not going to be stored in a cupboard then it can be wrapped in polythene sheeting.

Special racks can be made if there are a number of rollers because this stops the textiles from being flattened, which they will be if the

14   The drawer of an old wooden cabinet which has been lined with aluminium kitchen foil and acid-free tissue paper. The lace pieces have been rolled round paper tubes with cellophane round the outside so that the lace can be seen without undoing the roll. *Royal Scottish Museum*

rollers are stored on top of a flat surface. The racks can consist of two uprights with notches cut in them to take the ends of the rollers, or a pole can be put through the roller and the ends fitted into racks.

Most pieces of lace can also be rolled. In this case the rollers can be made from stiff paper or smaller cardboard tubes. The lace should be rolled in the same way as larger textiles but can be stored in a drawer or box. This method helps to keep the lace neat and makes it easier to store a quantity in a small space.

The methods described so far depend on being able to do good basic housekeeping to keep the rooms clean and up to a normal household standard outside the cupboards and boxes. If the collection is stored in attics or rooms which are not easy to keep clean then the garments will need protection from changes in temperature, dirt and insects.

Polythene bags have received bad reports from conservators, but for the private collector of limited means they are probably going to be essential. Polythene is inert so there is no danger of the material giving off harmful fumes or contaminating the contents in any way, and it is not harmful to humans either. The major objection to the bags is that because they are airtight when sealed a mini-environment is created which, as the air cannot circulate inside, provides ideal conditions for mould to grow. It is important not to allow this to happen because once the clothes are stained with mould it is difficult to remove the spots and it destroys the fabric. Polythene also attracts dust because of its static electricity, and the thicker the polythene the more dust it attracts. This makes the outside of the bags very dirty and it is difficult not to transfer some of the dirt to the contents.

However, the virtues of polythene are that it is able to give protection against insects and dirt in a more complete form than any other material, and because it is transparent it allows visual inspection of the contents which means that the clothes suffer less from handling. It is also much stronger than cellophane sheeting which is preferred by conservators but which tears very easily. Unlike polythene, cellophane is permeable which means that air can circulate through it.

One private collector has used polythene bags for over fifteen years to protect his collection from dirt and insects. The dresses have all been put on coat-hangers and then into a polythene bag, which is fastened round the neck of the hanger with a paper-covered wire closure. The fastening at the top is not completely airtight so that a certain amount of air can get in and out, but insects find it impossible to get inside. The encasing of each garment in its own bag has other advantages because it stops embroidery or lace being caught by fasteners on other dresses and, by trapping a certain amount of air, it acts as a cushion to prevent clothes becoming too creased even when packed very tightly together.

The bagged garments are then hung in wooden cupboards in the attics of the house and, because these are open to roof spaces where birds, bats and insects could quite easily get in, the cupboards are further protected by polythene sheets hung over them. Despite the great changes in temperature in the attic during the year there have been only about six cases of mould in this collection. This is quite a good record out of two thousand items.

Boxed pieces in this collection are also put into individual polythene bags but not sealed. The boxes are then stored on racking in the attic with polythene sheeting draped over the racks.

To discourage insects fresh newspaper was laid on top of the boxes and the shelves. When filling boxes with small, flat items take care not to fill them too full, because the polythene bags will then have all the air squeezed out and become moulded round the object. If the storage conditions are less than ideal, having these small items in individual bags means that they can be handled without getting them dirty.

Do remember that nothing can compensate for good house-keeping. Regular cleaning of rooms where costumes are stored, even attics, is essential if the things which do most harm to old textile pieces are to be controlled. Acid-free tissue paper should be changed frequently, for example whenever an object is taken out.

Insect damage from moths and carpet beetle is difficult to control unless regular cleaning is done. None of the products on the market, such as moth balls, should be used in close contact with costumes, but should always be hung inside the cupboard well away from the garments. Other chemicals such as paradichlorbenzene can be very harmful to humans and should on no account be handled by people or breathed in by them. One of the most effective discouragers of moth is fresh newspaper which can be used as a lining to cupboard bottoms and over boxes. Most modern clothes and carpets are moth-proofed so there should be little danger from the collector's own clothes and furnishings to their collection.

This chapter may well have made daunting reading. However, when a collection has been made at a certain cost in time and money it makes sense to protect it as well as possible. Time spent on storing items properly will not be wasted where costume and textiles are concerned.

CHAPTER FIVE

Conservation and repair

Conservation is the name given to the cleaning and repair of costumes and textiles in an effort to conserve them, that is in trying to slow down their decay. It should not be confused with the conservation of the natural environment. Restoration is not a term textile people like because it is not possible to restore a garment to its original state, nor is it desirable. Restoration implies that new parts will be made if any old ones are missing or too damaged to repair, and this is not practical in most costume repair work.

It is not advisable for the amateur to undertake conservation work because it has become a highly specialised field. Many of the changes which take place in the physical structure of a textile are complicated chemical reactions which need a good knowledge of chemistry to understand. Cleaning and washing textiles can set off a chain of reactions which may accelerate the decay of that piece, or cause even more problems than the treatment set out to cure. Much of what happens to a textile cannot be seen unlike, for example, the green excrescence which appears on bronzes and which is known as bronze disease. So the temptation of the costume collector to try major conservation of her own collection should be resisted.

Nevertheless, there are things the collector can do which will help the collection and not harm the items in it. But bear in mind that conservation work is usually an irreversible process and needs skill and great care if it is to be successful. So do not attempt anything beyond your capabilities or resources. When doing any conservation work time and calm are needed – it cannot be done in a hasty fashion.

Before attempting anything you would be well advised to read a good book on the subject. The best one so far available, written with the collector and country-house owner is mind, is *Caring for Textiles* by Karen Finch and Greta Putman (Barrie & Jenkins, 1977, and in America Watson-Guptill). This book also gives a list of suppliers of conservation materials and many drawings which illustrate the particular points.

SURFACE CLEANING

This is the simplest cleaning method. Many costumes and textiles, even embroideries, will benefit from being gently vacuum cleaned before any other method is tried. It is surprising how much dirt and dust can be removed this way and often the item will need no further cleaning.

For most pieces a small hand-held cleaner like those used for car interiors will be fine. So that the suction of the vacuum cleaner does not damage loose fibres or bead embroidery, cover the garment with a piece of smooth, plain, woven nylon net. This material has a very smooth weave and the nozzle of the cleaner does not come into contact with the garment. Less satisfactory is to put muslin over the cleaner nozzle, as the muslin has a rougher surface which could catch on the garment and cause damage to delicate pieces. Before using it extensively on any garment test a small area first.

Heavy clothes, particularly of a fairly recent date, can be brushed, but it should be done gently. Do not attempt this with old and delicate pieces, although crevices in heavy, raised embroidery may benefit from a very gentle brush with a fine sable hair brush to loosen the balls of dust.

When cleaning a garment that has beads or other loose decoration it is as well to empty the dust bag of the cleaner after use and check that nothing has been removed in the process. If the cleaning appears to be affecting the piece adversely then stop at once.

WASHING

Most white cotton and linen items such as children's and baby wear, underclothes, collars, cuffs and pelerines will benefit from a gentle wash if they are grubby. In the case of heavily starched garments it is, in fact, a good idea to remove the starch which can make the fibres very brittle and liable to break, as well as being a food source for insects. Some white clothes were 'dolly-blued' to enhance their whiteness, and the ultramarine-based powder sometimes used in this process may have left yellow patches which are impossible for the layman to shift.

When deciding whether or not to wash a white garment the strength of the material needs to be assessed. In very delicate muslins, particularly the whitework known as Ayrshire and used for babies' long-clothes, there may well be thin places. These are danger areas as is the embroidery itself which consists of holes filled in by needlework fillings. Fragile garments like this, once washed, should not be used again because they are unlikely to withstand repeated washings. But provided the fabric is not torn and great care is taken to support the object whilst it is being washed, then there should be no harm in doing it once.

Coloured garments are much more difficult to wash. Each dye must be tested first to ensure it does not run, since many early dyes are liable to do just this when wet. Printed cottons and linens are often all right because they were usually made as washable fabrics in the first place, but the layman should not attempt to wash silk or woollen garments, even if they are all of one colour.

Dresses can have other problems which make washing hazardous. They are often lined with whale or steel bones inserted in them and it is not always easy to remove linings without destroying an integral part of the garment. If both lining and dress are very dirty then washing can trap the dirt between the two layers and also leave stains. When the lining is of a different fabric from the garment, or in any piece where there is more than one type of fabric used, then do not wash it.

If you do decide to wash a particular item then there are certain things you will have to assemble first. A flat vessel is needed for the actual washing, large enough to let the piece lie flat if possible. Photographers' developing trays are good for this, or any suitable container in polythene or plastic. For larger items various improvised washing tanks can be constructed using heavy duty polythene sheeting with some pieces of wood or plastic tubing to form the sides.

Soft water is the ideal for washing. In some parts of Britain, the tap water is soft enough but in hard water areas a proprietary water softener, like Calgon, should be used. This must be thoroughly dissolved in the water first before any garments are added.

The water should not be too hot, around 38°C (100°F) is the limit – more or less blood heat. Avoid sharp changes in temperature when washing and on no account should old textiles be boiled or bleached, as both processes are very harmful.

Instead of ordinary household washing powders you must use something like Synperonic N, formerly known as Lissapol N, which should be diluted first to a 1 per cent solution (1 cc of SN to 1 litre of water). If this is difficult to find then a neutral coloured dish-washing liquid without optical whiteners is acceptable. You might need to use this at a slightly higher strength, such as 2 cc to 1 litre of water. For the final rinse use distilled water which can be bought from the chemist. Do not use that supplied by garages for car batteries, as it may not be pure enough.

The diluted washing agent should be used in very small quantities in the warm water. Place the garment to be washed on a piece of nylon net or a polythene sheet which is larger in size, so that the clothing is not directly handled when wet. Then lower the net into the water and, using a small sponge, press gently up and down on the garment to help release the dirt, but never rub or squeeze it. If the water gets very dirty you can do a second wash.

Rinse the garment with barely warm running water. If you are using soft tap water then a hair-washing spray attachment is a useful aid. Several rinses will be necessary until there is no more soap solution to come out and the water runs clear. A final rinse in distilled water is important because impurities in ordinary water can remain behind and cause things like iron mould.

The next step is drying and, because ironing is not particularly good for old textiles, they should be dried as flat as possible. This is difficult with costumes. Flat textiles which are heavy can have some of the excess water taken out by rolling in a towel or blotting with absorbent material, otherwise fabrics should be allowed to dry naturally away from sun, bright light or artificial heat. Items should be smoothed into shape on a flat surface. A clean Formica-topped table is quite good for this and for smaller pieces a sheet of glass, or Formica-covered board, can be used. If the wet item is carefully smoothed flat on this type of surface, with all air bubbles removed, then virtually no ironing will be needed.

For lace or embroidered pieces, where the edges have to be straightened out, a slightly different process is used. A piece of softboard or cork is covered in melinex film or polythene and the piece can then be pinned to this after being gently eased into shape. The small picots at the edges and any central holes which need to be kept straight should be pinned, using white brass pins. The pins do not go through the lace but through the holes so that the fabric is not damaged. Steel pins will rust so should not be used.

If a garment has to be ironed then do this at a cool temperature and not above 100°C, usually about the lowest setting marked on an iron. It is a good idea to put a piece of fine muslin over the garment first and iron over this to avoid scorching. Make sure that the bottom of the iron is clean and the ironing board is covered in a clean, smooth, white fabric; cotton sheeting, cambric or Habutai silk are all suitable. Some stains are set at fairly low temperatures, so beware of ironing a garment which is not clean because the heat can set any stains or dirt into the fabric and make them almost impossible to remove. Creases can be taken out by using a steam valet which works in much the same way as steam from a kettle, but is more controlled.

There are many spots found on textiles which will not come out with washing. These stubborn stains should be left and no attempt should be made to try and bleach them out or use other techniques. Even conservators will not risk trying to remove some spots. The collector must appreciate that it is just not possible to restore a garment to its original pristine freshness. It cannot be emphasised too much that the chemical and physical changes which fabrics undergo in both manufacture and use are irreversible, and there is no point in asking the conservator to do the impossible.

DRY-CLEANING

This is the most drastic method of all because it involves a lot of mechanical action as well as the cleaning fluid. Not all items can be dry-cleaned since some fabrics are affected by the solvents used.

Although one or two museums have their own machines, most institutions use local cleaners who are prepared to take special care of old pieces. As in washing, the dyes have to be tested to make sure they will not run in the cleaning fluid. Most commercial cleaners in Britain use either Arklone or Perklone, the 'A' and 'P' found on dress labels. Both fluids have to be used professionally in specially designed machinery, although this does mean that there is less control of the cleaning process by the operator than when hand washing is used.

Try to avoid coin-operated or fast service cleaners as the fluid is only filtered in these machines. For the proper cleaning of old textiles it is better to use clean fluid in a machine which re-distills it so that all impurities have been taken out. This is why a local cleaner who is prepared to take trouble with old textiles is essential. Firms to look out for are those which clean wedding dresses and elaborate evening gowns. For a dry-cleaning firm clean solvent costs money and time which makes the price high.

A dry-cleaning machine consists basically of a drum which re-volves, tossing the clothes so that they tumble around. For safe cleaning of old textiles an oscillating motion is preferable, merely swishing the fluid over the pieces lying at the base of the drum.

What will dry-clean?
All modern garments which have their cleaning instructions inside should be safe to dry-clean. Most men's clothes made of wool and such things as army uniforms will clean well, as will women's woollen dresses, though the linings should be checked. Most silks can be dry-cleaned but take care when considering eighteenth-century pieces: anything in a fragile state will probably not be suitable. Small embroideries and samplers can often be cleaned by this method too.

The responsibility for cleaning will rest ultimately with the owner and the firm will probably not accept responsibility, pointing out some of the risks involved. Ask for clean not filtered fluid and do not have any finishes such as re-texturing. A certain amount of prepara-tion is necessary before cleaning and this must be done by the collector.

Buttons should be protected by wrapping loose-weave muslin round each one. Wrap tassels and other hanging bits in muslin, and embroidery, especially bead-work, should have pieces of muslin lightly tacked over it to prevent any beads from coming off and being lost. Worn edges might need some muslin sewn over them to stop any friction during the cleaning process. The muslin used is loosely woven so the fluid can get through but it will stop any abrasion caused by the mechanical action in the machine.

After the various parts have been treated in this way the whole garment should be sewn firmly between two pieces of muslin or nylon net with the stitching going round the outline of the piece and not through it. The whole garment will thus be in a bag. This will stop the arms or legs from getting tangled and help to make a heavier parcel which will cling to the sides of the drum and stop it from being thrown around. Once the garment has been cleaned, air it thoroughly before storing to get rid of any remaining traces of the fluid.

It is possible to dry-clean small items, such as samplers, at home using white spirit (BS 245), which is a clean form of turpentine. It is known as Stoddart's solvent in America. This is extremely inflammable and must be used in a very well-ventilated room, or preferably out of doors on a fine day well away from any building. As with washing, test each colour for colour fastness before you proceed. Use an orange stick with a small amount of cotton wool at the tip which has been dipped in the spirit. Apply this to each colour separately and then blot dry. If any colour has transferred itself to the blotting material this means that the dye is soluble in the spirit and cannot be cleaned this way.

If the test is negative lay the sampler flat in a polythene tray which is large enough to hold it, not forgetting to support it on a piece of nylon net or polythene sheeting. Then pour the spirit over the sampler and agitate the surface gently with a soft brush. This should take about fifteen minutes and if the piece is very dirty you can try a second bath. When it is clean lift it out using the net backing and blot off any surplus solvent. Dry it in a well-ventilated place out of direct sunlight and well away from naked flames and lighted cigarettes. Do not tip the dirty solvent down the kitchen sink; it can be kept for cleaning paint brushes, or if a very large quantity accumulates a local painter and decorator might be prepared to dispose of it. On no account should you empty it into the waste water drainage system. White spirit is only suitable for small pieces as it evaporates and the quantity necessary for larger pieces would make the process expensive.

REPAIR

The general repair of textiles is as important as conservation. The skills of plain sewing that were taught in the past are no longer generally known and the less skilled person who attempts this kind of work can do great damage. Repairing old textiles demands both sensitivity and competence in the skills of hand sewing. Machine sewing is rarely suitable for this type of work.

The limitations on successful hand sewing today are a lack of fine needles and threads, and the lack of similar fabrics. If repair work is to be done new fabrics must match, or be in sympathy with, the

15 Detail of the end of the sleeve of a baby's first shirt, eighteenth century. This shows the fine hand sewing which was a feature of baby clothes of this period. Adults clothes were usually not so well sewn until the early nineteenth century. The tiny back stitches along the wristband are almost regular enough to be mistaken for machine sewing. *Royal Scottish Museum, Shambellie 1504*

original. Using old fabrics can be difficult because they may well not be strong enough.

Specialist fabric shops, particularly in London, have good plain silks which can be dyed to match the antique textile. It can be difficult to match some weaves though, and the old type of silk taffeta was very hard to find at one time. It is also not easy to match the old watered, corded silks. For printed and painted clothes the only solution is to paint the pattern onto a fabric with a similar ground.

Repair work, like conservation, cannot restore the garment to its former condition, only improve its looks. Conservators are usually keen that repairs, whilst not being obvious to the eye at a distance, are apparent when viewed close to because they do not intend to deceive. It is important to clarify what has been restored so that any study of a particular piece in the future will reveal exactly what is genuine.

When restoring a bonnet, for instance, which has lost all its trimmings use materials which are sympathetic and in keeping with the period. Too often nylon satin ribbons in modern shades are used and they look incongruous. It is the measure of a good repairer to match repairs to the period of the object so that it looks right. This can bring the repairer into conflict with designers who want to achieve a visual effect which will appeal to a modern audience. So bear this in mind when doing display work.

What can be safely repaired? What should be repaired? It goes without saying that all buttons and other fastenings should be re-sewn if they have become detached, or replacements provided where possible. Fastenings which are out of sight can be replaced by similar modern ones if there are no old ones to be had. This is important if the dress is to be on display because pinning can cause problems and it is safer to sew on new fasteners than to rely on pins. Zip fasteners should not be replaced by modern nylon ones if they are in an obvious place. Those which are hidden under the arm in the side seam can probably be replaced by using press-studs or hooks and eyes.

When fastenings are decorative then it can be more difficult to replace them. It is possible to make a replica of most buttons and some, like thread buttons, can easily be made to match. Cloth buttons, if they match the dress fabric, can sometimes be replaced by taking some material from the hem or side seams and covering a blank. If you cannot provide a good replica then the replacement should be put in as inconspicuous a place as possible, or somewhere where it can be covered up – by an arm, for example – when it is displayed.

Lace and other trimmings are important to a garment's appearance. If some part of the trimming is missing do try to replace it. The machine laces of the nineteenth and early twentieth centuries are very plentiful and fairly cheap, making replacement easy. But do not use these laces on eighteenth-century dresses to make sleeve frills. If you cannot find lace of the right period it is much better to make some out of modern silk gauze or fine muslin.

Ribbons are difficult because it is now almost impossible to find the marvellous patterned variety, or the wide ones so often used on Victorian bonnets. Nylon satin and velvet ribbons are not right and can detract from the look of the bonnet. It is worth taking the time and trouble to hunt out good quality modern ribbons at the few stores or specialist shops which still sell them, even though they will be expensive.

When conservation has been unable to deal with a spot it is sometimes possible to put a patch over it using matching material. Otherwise it can be hidden when the garment is displayed. For instance, many brides spill wine down the front of their wedding dresses, but the hands can be arranged to hold the bouquet over the marks which usually occur at the top of the skirt.

If you are contemplating patching remember that this has to be sewn. Many fabrics are so tightly woven it is not easy to push a needle through them, and a coarse modern needle can leave an unsightly hole. Twenty years ago there was a great vogue for 'sticky net', a nylon net treated with a solution which became sticky when heated. The net was applied by ironing and was used extensively to strengthen weak parts of textiles. Recently, however, the full implications of the chemical damage done to fabrics by the solution were revealed and it is no longer considered satisfactory – so please do not use it. If the hole is unobtrusive then leave it alone. Some holes need mending if they endanger the textile, making it liable to be caught or snagged even when handled carefully. For very fine muslins a patch over a small hole may be very obtrusive and a good darn would be better. Remember that when a garment is displayed it must be strong enough to withstand the strains of exhibition, and repair helps to achieve this.

Whether you use a patch or a darn, or decide to leave the hole, will depend on two things. If the garment is to be displayed then the look is important and camouflage is better, but if it is weak then any work you do on it may weaken it further by stressing the fabric. A complete lining for a flat textile which is weak would be better than patching or darning, but for clothes such a solution is not always possible.

Shattered silk linings to dresses are totally uneconomic to repair both in time and in materials. The best solution is to find a fabric of a similar weight, either in polyester or silk, and cut a replacement lining using the old one as a pattern (see pages 76–78 on taking a pattern). The correct weight of fabric is important otherwise the dress will lose its underlying shape which the lining supplied and the fall of the gown will be ruined when it is displayed. If necessary a new lining can be dyed to match using Dylon dye.

Shattered silk dresses are more of a problem. The best advice is never to accept one into your collection. However, if it has sentimental or great historic value then it is best to get a professional conservator to do the work, but be prepared for a heavy bill.

16   The inside of a woman's jacket of about 1907 showing the cream satin lining starting to disintegrate. This is the condition known as *shattered silk. Royal Scottish Museum, 1966.735*

When repairing tears in side seams or sewing in new fasteners match the type of stitch to the original. Many hand sewn seams on dress skirts use running stitches while backstitch was used for bodices. Where machine stitching has come undone repair it by hand sewing, using the old stitch holes where possible.

White collars and cuffs were usually just tacked inside the neck and sleeve edges because they were regularly removed for washing. There is no need to sew them in more firmly.

Certain accessories pose further problems for repairers. Parasols with split covers are not easy to handle but again, before having it repaired professionally think about the cost.

Re-ribboning brisé fans, where short lengths of ribbon join the carved pieces which form both leaf and stick, needs patience and practice as well as the correct ribbon. This is obtainable and the Fan Circle keeps stocks for its members. Broken guards can be stuck, but remounting a leaf or repairing it can be much more difficult. 'Sticky net' was often used for this but apart from the danger this poses to the fabric it also has a tendency to stick to other things, making it difficult to open a fan once it has been treated.

No sticky transparent tape, such as Sellotape, should be used on either the textiles or paper parts of a fan, or any other costume item. Use of this in the past may well have left nasty patches of glue which are difficult to remove safely.

Shoes, like other leather pieces, can benefit from the application of some BM leather dressing. Use it sparingly and rub it in well, repeating the process if necessary. Do not use this on patent or suede leathers and avoid modern shoe polishes or sprays. Fabric uppers are difficult to treat because shoes are usually lined and various glues have been used in their making. Vacuuming will help to remove dust. If leather dressing is used on the leather heels of fabric shoes take great care not to get it on the uppers. Northampton Museum issues a free leaflet on the cleaning and care of old shoes which the collector will find very helpful.

Whenever conservation or repair work is carried out you should make notes on the treatment used and either keep them in a separate file or add them to the inventory. This will help if the garment needs further work so that a check can be made on what has already been done. It will also help if any damage or change is noticed afterwards so that similar treatment can be avoided in the future. Any replacement parts that have been made should also be noted. If a lining is replaced, for example, then it is a good idea to keep a small piece of the old one in the file, so that the original can be checked by any future student.

CHAPTER SIX

Making an inventory

A comprehensive inventory of objects is extremely important today for the efficient running of any museum. It was not always so, and even twenty years ago it was still possible to find small public museums which had poor or non-existent inventories. Modern computer techniques have been introduced in some areas to cope with the sheer volume of material which over a hundred years of collecting has produced.

Inventories are extremely important for any collection which is available to the public – this includes libraries and archives as well as museums. There are several reasons for this, the most obvious being to provide a list of items for the public to see; a library catalogue is probably the one with which most people are familiar. Security is crucial for museums and without an inventory it is impossible to know exactly what is held.

The making of an inventory is known by various names, but in museums it is often called registration. For legal reasons museums usually possess bound books called registers into which each object is entered as it has been acquired. It was considered that a bound, handwritten volume would be less easy to tamper with than a loose-leaf register or a card index.

Today many museums have two separate systems, using a bound book to record, very briefly, the objects and their donors as they are received, and a larger bound or loose-leaf book, or card system, in which detailed information and descriptions are written at leisure. Specially designed cards can be used to record the information which can eventually be transferred to a computer.

A well-run museum also needs several auxiliary inventories or indexes to help it function. The most obvious is a location index, which lists all the objects by number and records exactly where each is stored. A further index of each gallery and store records by case, cupboard, drawer and shelf what is to be found there. To help answer the various inquiries that come in, indexes by country, site, type or technique are needed.

All these secondary listings, though, are dependent on the main inventory in which the identity of the object, its date and a full description of it are made. This is a very important part of a curator's work because by the time this has been completed there should be little else to be discovered about the item.

The making of an inventory by a private collector is no less necessary. First there is the security aspect which is becoming increasingly important. Photographs or drawings alone cannot give a complete view of an object, it must be accompanied by a written description and this is best done with the object to hand, not by recollection. Inventories also help in other ways; for example in bequests. The collector will know which is her second best sack dress, to be left to a favourite niece, but does her executor? An inventory can also give a sense of enjoyment because as the collection grows it will be less easy to remember details of various pieces. If these are written down at the time of acquisition then the details will remain fresh.

Making an inventory is not difficult once the basic concepts are understood. It is probably easier for the collector to use loose-leaf sheets or large cards which can be typed, rather than bound books which have to be handwritten. Printed heading put onto paper or card help to make the inventory look neater and remind the collector of the sequence of the information needed. Some form of storage for these cards must also be considered and you may decide to make a copy to lodge in the bank. Many museums now microfilm their registers and have them stored outside their own building in a safe place in case the original is destroyed.

NUMBERING

The basic idea of an inventory is to list all items so that they can be recognised individually. To begin with museums give each object an accession number which is unique to that object. This numbering is sometimes done serially – 1, 2, 3 – or, more usually today, by a series of numbers incorporating the year, such as 1981.1, 1.1981, or 981.1. They sometimes use a prefix to denote a department in a large museum, such as T1981.1 for textiles. Whatever system is used the idea is the same – each object has a number which is exclusive to itself in that collection. 1981.1 represents the first object acquired in 1981 and the next object would be 1981.2, even if it was given by the same person. Numbering is not meant to be a complicated system and many museums use the same one. This is unlikely to cause confusion when objects are lent to exhibitions from various museums, but there is now a scheme in publications whereby the museum's initials prefix the number.

For the private collector a simple serial numbering system will no doubt be adequate. But if the items are to be lent to exhibitions fairly frequently then the initials of the owner might be incorporated, for example JMKl.

Once a number has been allocated then it has to be attached to the object in some way. For costume and textiles this is generally done by writing the number on narrow white tape in marking ink and then sewing the tape to the garment. Never mark the garment directly with marking ink, biro or felt tip pen as this can cause damage. The tape should be sewn in a place where it can be seen quickly and precludes unnecessary handling. The inside neck of dresses and coats is a good place, but avoid the hems of skirts. For large textiles a lower corner at the back is probably the best location. Each piece in an ensemble must have the number sewn on it, for example if there is a separate bodice, skirt and belt all three should have the number put on.

For shoes and other items made of non-textile materials the number can be painted on using a fine brush and black or white enamel paints. Shoes should be marked on the bottom on the instep but the number should not cover any decoration or marks. Parasols should be marked on the part of the handle that is covered when the parasol is closed, or else the number can be written on a tape and looped round the framework. Fans can have their numbers painted on the reverse of the front guard, and if it is done very neatly it will not be offensive to the eye. Metalwork should not have the number engraved but painted on.

When a garment is to be displayed and the number is in too obvious a place then the tape can be unpicked and sewn somewhere else for the duration of the exhibition, but do not remove the number completely even for a short time. Pieces lent to an exhibition need to have their owners' identifying numbers inside to stop any disagreements arising over ownership at the end of the show.

THE FORMAT OF AN INVENTORY

The thing to remember when deciding on a format for an inventory is to make each section clearly visible. This allows a quick look at relevant sections of several cards without having to search each one for the information required.

Always put at the top the most important things such as the number, what the garment is and its date. The hardest part of making an inventory is deciding what the piece is and its date and this will be discussed later.

It is essential to put down how many pieces there are under each number. For example, an 1870s' dress might have a separate bodice and skirt, a belt and a separate back bustle drape, which would make four pieces in all. Anything which can be removed should be numbered and counted for its safety.

In addition note which sex the item is made for and whether it is for an adult, a child or a baby, if this is known. These can be written out 'Male/Female/Adult/Child/Baby' and then the relevant ones circled or the non-relevant deleted.

Some kind of measurement is useful. This need not be exhaustive of every part but enough to help in identification. Flat textiles can be measured in both length and width. Costumes can have their neck to hem length recorded and it might be of interest to take waist measurements. Each type of object should be measured in the same place. It is also a good idea to be consistent in the use of imperial or metric systems. When using metric, though, it is much more sensible to use centimetres for textile items, even if these are officially discouraged in favour of millimetres. This is because cloth can stretch so easily as to make accurate measurement to millimetres useless. With inches it is only necessary to go to the nearest quarter-inch and usually the nearest half-inch will be adequate for most purposes. Non-textile items like fans can be measured more accurately.

The materials from which garments are made are a very important feature in the description of the piece. When you describe fabric it is useful to take a guess at whether it is wool, silk, linen, cotton or a man-made material. But a question mark should always be put after anything about which the compiler is uncertain because this warns her, or any other researcher in the future, that there is some doubt about this area of identification.

Colour is a difficult subject. Many men are slightly colour blind and this alters their perception of certain colours. Several attempts have been made to use some kind of standard colour system, such as British Standard Colours, but they have all proved unworkable. The easiest is probably to describe colours very simply using the main colour first, such as black, white, blue, green, red, yellow, mauve/ purple. The depth of colour can be indicated by light, medium or dark, with dull or bright added if it helps. If the colour looks like a well-known one such as Wedgwood blue then this can be included, but it should be an additional piece of information and put in brackets.

Patterned fabrics should have a brief description of their design. If you use terms like acanthus or paisley, make sure that you really understand the term. If you are expert enough to recognise printing techniques – block, plate, roller, screen – then this can be added.

The original names of the fabrics are probably long since forgotten and, unless definitely known, should be used with caution. There have been many changes in fabrics over the years and often the same name is applied to a different fabric at a later date. Nevertheless, the collector should learn to recognise such distinctive finishes as satin, watered and corded. Otherwise phrases such as light-weight silk, knobbly-surfaced fancy-weave wool, are much better than an incorrect guess at a technical term which could be very misleading. It is important for the collector not to attempt more than she feels competent to do, or else she may well never make an inventory.

Trimmings should also be noted. These include ribbons, lace and embroidery. Again, colours and fibre should be given if known and an attempt made to identify the lace as hand- or machine-made.

A full description of the garment can start at the neck and work towards the hem. If there is a separate bodice and skirt begin with the bodice. Everything should be noted including the lining and the fastenings. If the technical terms are known for such things as stitches then these can be added, and it is important to note whether a garment is hand- or machine-sewn. During this process the dress must be thoroughly investigated and turned inside out in case anything which might help with dating is left unseen.

If any garment has a dressmaker's label or a shop label sewn inside then this also should be noted. They started to come in in the 1860s but hats and shoes carried them in the eighteenth century. Finally any information about the original wearer of the garment must be recorded; when it was worn and where, and where it was bought and for how much. This is known as provenance and is of historical importance. Too often this type of information is disregarded by collectors and sale catalogues rarely include it, no doubt because many sellers wish to remain anonymous. Whenever a piece is sold from a collection this knowledge must go with it; on no account should objects lose their provenance.

For a collector's own information a further section can be made recording when she acquired the piece and who gave it to her, or where and for how much she bought it.

Drawings and photographs can be put on the back of the sheets. If a separate conservation file is not kept then this information can be added either on the back or on a separate sheet clipped to the main one.

To help illustrate the format described above here is a detailed description of an actual dress.

Number: 1981.557A&B   **Object:** Dress   **Date:** about 1870
No. of pieces: 3   **Female, Adult.**
Material: Pale cream silk, warp printed in shades of mauve with small flower sprays (chiné silk).
Trimmings: White tulle; deep mauve corded silk; machine-made blonde lace; Honiton lace; clear and opaque glass beads.
Size: day bodice: centre back length 57 cm
                  A. skirt: centre back length 170 cm
                  B. evening bodice: centre back length 30 cm

DESCRIPTION:
Day bodice: Chiné silk bodice ends at natural waist at front, cut with coat tails at back. V-neck at front trimmed inside with silk net, and on the outside with lace and pleated mauve silk ending in two rosettes. Open down centre front, fastened by 5 brass hooks. Draw ribbon round neck. Coat tails edged with mauve silk ending in a wide bow with long ends. Smaller bow at centre back waist. Half belt fastening at centre front. Piped armhole seam. Sleeves to elbow finished with pleated mauve silk, a puff of tulle, another band of silk with a bow, and a frill of lace. Lined in glazed white cotton. 7 bones. Silk ribbon waist ties. 4 brass hooks to attach bodice to skirt. Machine-sewn.
A. Skirt: A trained skirt in the chiné silk. Centre front panel of white net over white silk taffeta, caught up in puffs by four broad bands of

mauve silk with a bow at centre front of each band. Down each side of the panel is a 'rever' of silk edged with mauve silk and lace. Waistband of cream-twilled satin tape. Skirt cartridge pleated at centre back. Open at centre back, fastened by 3 brass hooks and eyes. Brass eyes for bodice hooks. Inside, centre panel is backed by stiff gauze. Broad tape tie on each side of panel to hold fullness to the

17 The dress described on page 73 The pointers to dating this dress are the fairly plain skirt with no overskirt and little or no bustle. This is very like the skirts of the late 1860s. Central panels in skirts can be found in fashion plates for 1870, and they get more elaborate. The sleeves of the day bodice, shown here, are not as wide or as heavily ornamented as those of the early 1870s. The natural waistline and the square neckline were both popular in 1870. It is not a particularly up-to-the-minute dress but it is a very elegant one for a young matron. *Royal Scottish Museum, 1981.557&A*

back. Glazed cotton pocket in right side seam. Deep hem of stiffened muslin. Machine-sewn.

B. Evening bodice: Of chiné silk, ends at the natural waist with a point centre front and back. Low wide neckline filled in by a shallow V of net over taffeta. Above is an edging of Honiton lace with narrow black velvet ribbon threaded through. Mock collar with pointed ends at centre back and front and on shoulders, with a white taffeta band edged with bias strips of mauve taffeta sewn in small box pleats. Below this is a hanging band of clear glass beads with loops of opaque bugle beads. Tiny cap sleeves of two rows of net frilling over two bands of mauve taffeta. The over sleeve is slit on top and trimmed to match the collar. Honiton lace and ribbon edging. Open down centre front, fastened by 5 large round clear glass bobble buttons and worked buttonholes. Waist seam piped in mauve taffeta. Lined in glazed cotton. 8 bones. Silk ribbon waist ties. Machine-sewn.

Alterations: None to either bodice but skirt has some resewn seams, e.g. either side centre panel. Trimming of evening bodice does not match skirt; the mauve taffeta is lighter in shade than the corded

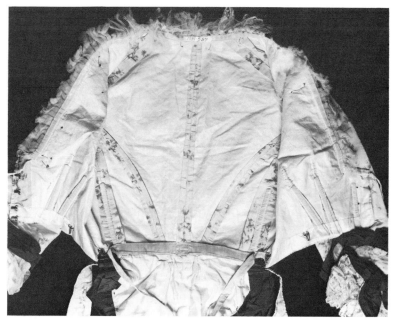

18 The inside of the bodice of the dress in photo 17, showing the typical construction of the bodices of this period

silk. Possibly the day bodice is made out of front widths of skirt which originally matched the evening bodice.

Condition: Net frilling at neck disintegrating.

Label: None

Details of wearer: Belonged to Miss Georgina Graham Bell, 1840–1914, who married Thomas Ellis Steuart, an Edinburgh lawyer, in 1866.

Acquired from: Given

The dress chosen is a fairly standard one for the late nineteenth century to illustrate the type of information which can be recorded. It does not have to be as detailed or as cryptically written as this, but can be even more detailed if the compiler wishes. Recording in this way assumes that another reader will know some of the terms used, 'piped' for example. To assume complete ignorance of costume, though, can lead to a totally unreadable account. Ideally the description should be able to give anyone with some knowledge of costume history a mental picture of what the piece looks like. It is difficult for the compiler to know whether they have achieved this, and in a museum there is rarely time to find out.

TAKING A PATTERN

Taking a scale pattern from an antique dress is not hard but it can be time consuming, and if you do not already have a knowledge of dressmaking it is not recommended. There is more than one way of taking a pattern but the method described here is probably easier than most. A dress should never be taken to pieces to get a pattern; there is no need for this and it destroys the garment.

Before starting assemble all the necessary items: a large table or flat surface to spread the dress out on, a soft cover for the table, graph paper on which to draw the pattern, in either metric or imperial measure depending on preference. If you choose to work in inches the graph paper should ideally be divided into eighths of an inch rather than tenths or twelfths. A flexible dressmaker's tape, a retractable metal tape measure, fine white brass pins and butterfly pins, sharpened pencils, a soft rubber and a ruler are also needed. Those with long sight will find a large magnifying glass essential.

For a first effort it is a good idea to choose something simple – an early nineteenth-century dress is probably the best choice. Dresses from the 1870s onwards are far too complicated and the 1930s' bias-cut dresses will be best left until the collector has had some experience of taking a pattern. If there is nothing suitable in the collection then you will find it simpler to take the pattern of a modern dress in your own wardrobe than to attempt a difficult antique one.

Once everything is assembled mark out the graph paper ready to use – large sheets are preferable. Construct a grid, or base lines, by using one bottom corner and marking it 0. The outer lines up and along should then be marked off 8, 16, 24 if $\frac{1}{8}$ in. graph paper is used, or 10, 20 and so on if metric is used. Each square marked by the heavy lines on the paper measures 1 in. and represents an 8-in. square. Each small square is $\frac{1}{8}$ in. square and represents 1 in. When drawn out the pattern will be to the scale $\frac{1}{8}$ in.:1 in. Metric paper is normally divided into millimetres and those unaccustomed to the metric system, or to using graph paper, may find it difficult to use at first as the divisions are rather small.

The next stage is to look carefully at the dress and decide which is the simplest section to start with. For an early nineteenth-century dress this will probably be the skirt. If it has a straight waistline with a gathered skirt, then this will be the best part to draw first. Measure the height from waist to hem edge and mark this by a dot on the vertical line of the paper. Next, measure one width, selvedge to selvedge, and mark this also by a dot but on the horizontal line. Then using a ruler draw up from the horizontal mark to a point level with the vertical mark and then another line across to join it. If there are several identical pieces the one drawn out should be marked 'Cut 2', or however many there are. But if one piece has an opening in it for the back fastening or a pocket slit, this should be drawn out separately and the openings marked. It is a good idea to do a small drawing showing the sequence of widths round the skirt to help when making up the pattern.

Next the way the skirt is attached to the bodice should be marked. Many dresses only have gathering at the centre back so that the fullness is concentrated into a very small area. This should be noted by arrows pointing to each end of the area to be gathered up and the length noted thus: 'Gather in to 3 inches.' Mark the depth of the hem by a dotted line. No hem or seam allowances are given when drawing out a pattern. The pieces should also be marked 'Front', 'Back', 'Side'.

Bodices are usually the hardest part to draw because they are shaped. The simplest part is usually the back because there are no darts here and the shaping is done by the seams. The first thing to establish on any piece, which is not just a straight width of fabric, is the grain line. This is the direction of the warps, the vertical threads in the woven cloth. If a piece is not cut using the straight grain as the basis it is said to be cut on the cross, or bias, of the fabric. It is this that gives the floating line to the dresses of the 1930s and makes them cling to the body. Bias cutting was not an invention of the 1930s but was used to its greatest effect then. The front bodices of dresses of the 1800s are sometimes bias cut, and so are some of the tight-fitting bodices of the mid-nineteenth century.

If a pattern has a strong vertical line such as woven stripes then it is easy to find the straight grain. If not, the warp has to be found and marked and you may need a magnifying glass if the fabric is very tightly woven. Once found the vertical threads should be marked by a line of fine pins from top to bottom of the piece, all following the same warp thread. If the piece is cut on the cross, mark the grain line and treat it in the same way as a piece cut on the straight. A tape measure needs to be placed along the line of pins.

Another base line may have to be drawn out above the skirt for another section of the pattern. Draw out the bodice on the paper in sequence; the right-hand side of the back should go on the right of the left-hand piece, otherwise it will not be so easy to follow. As the straight grain will come somewhere in the middle of the piece you are drawing, leave space on the paper for drawing either side of the vertical line.

Measurements are taken from the line of pins marking the straight grain at right angles to points on the outer edges of the bodice, such as the armholes and the side seams. After they have been plotted on the paper join up the dots. Do not draw them with a ruler as there may well be slight curves in the line which help to give shape to the bodice. Each piece should be treated in the same way until the whole of the bodice, including the sleeves, has been plotted on the paper. Balancing marks need to be put in so that the exact place where each piece joins another is clear.

Rough pattern of a simple late 1830s' dress which took two hours to do. Because of the gathering and ruching on the sleeve the length is uncertain but this would be corrected when a cotton toile is cut. The bodice front is cut on the cross and it proved difficult to draw because a decorative piece from the shoulder obscured the bust dart. A weaving fault helped to indicate the grain line which is why the right front was chosen. For a view of the inside of this bodice see photo 19.

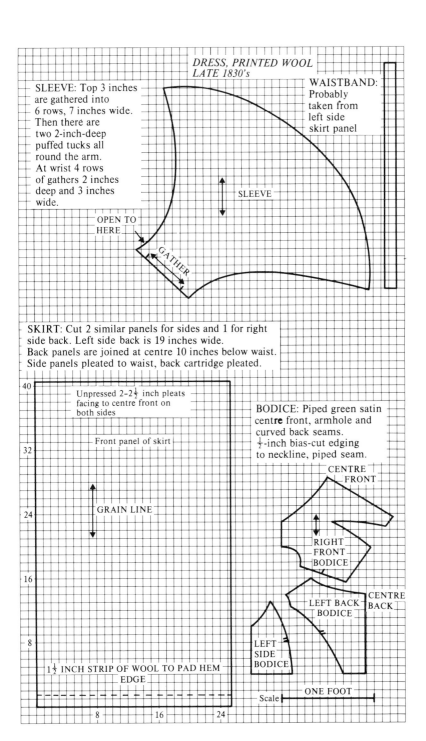

DRESS, PRINTED WOOL
LATE 1830's

SLEEVE: Top 3 inches
are gathered into
6 rows, 7 inches wide.
Then there are
two 2-inch-deep
puffed tucks all
round the arm.
At wrist 4 rows
of gathers 2 inches
deep and 3 inches
wide.

WAISTBAND:
Probably
taken from
left side
skirt panel

SLEEVE

OPEN TO
HERE

GATHER

SKIRT: Cut 2 similar panels for sides and 1 for right
side back. Left side back is 19 inches wide.
Back panels are joined at centre 10 inches below waist.
Side panels pleated to waist, back cartridge pleated.

40

Unpressed 2–2½ inch pleats
facing to centre front on
both sides

BODICE: Piped green satin
centre front, armhole and
curved back seams.
½-inch bias-cut edging
to neckline, piped seam.

Front panel of skirt

32

CENTRE
FRONT

24

GRAIN LINE

RIGHT
FRONT
BODICE

16

LEFT BACK
BODICE

CENTRE
BACK

8

LEFT
SIDE
BODICE

1½ INCH STRIP OF WOOL TO PAD HEM
EDGE

ONE FOOT

Scale

8   16   24

When taking a pattern ignore the trimmings since it is the basic structure that is being recorded. When that is finished you can mark the exact placing of the trimmings by dotted lines. They should also be measured or drawn unless only the basic pattern of the dress is required.

If the fabric is very closely woven, like silk taffeta or very heavy brocade, using pins to mark the grain line might be damaging, so a fixed tape measure marking the grain would be better. For this you need a soft cloth under the dress so that a flexible dressmaker's tape can be placed along the grain line and then pinned to it beyond the neckline. The other end can be pinned in the same way or weighted down. As the tape has to be kept taut and on the grain line it must be firmly fixed.

Measurements are taken from the tape in the same way as they were from the line of pins. But remember that only one side of the tape represents the straight grain, so that when measuring from the other side of the tape its width must be included otherwise you will be ½ in. out.

To check the pattern it is a good idea to make up half of it in a firm white cotton cloth. The pattern will have to be drawn out on the cotton at the correct size. The made-up section should resemble the original and if it does not then there is something wrong with the pattern and it needs checking.

To take a pattern of a unique garment, or to make one which is a complete record, demands a lot of time. In the case of something like a sixteenth-century doublet it may take several days. All the minute details of trimming and lining and construction have to be noted and checked. However, it is highly unlikely that the majority of collectors would be able to do patterns of such unique items, as most museums would not let anyone but the most reputable scholar take a pattern from their rare pieces. This is understandable because taking a pattern means a garment is handled and too much of this, however careful, will not be good for it. Once a pattern has been taken of these rare items by the museum staff or a scholar they are unlikely to allow anyone else to do it again. If the pattern is published then it will be available for everyone to see and to copy for plays or reproduction garments.

For collectors there are several reasons why patterns of their own pieces are valuable, even if they are not going to make clothes for a play, for their children to dress up in, or reproduction clothes for a house or museum. Taking a pattern means understanding the dressmaking and construction techniques of the past and will help to give a better understanding of the pieces. A flat pattern can be easier to understand than a made-up garment and makes comparisons between dresses easier. With the trimmings removed the basic construction is visible and can help in dating pieces by comparing similar patterns.

Patterns should be carefully stored in envelopes or files and kept with the inventory cards if possible. If the pattern is of a garment not your own collection then date order is quite a good way of storing this type of information.

PHOTOGRAPHY

The photography of private collections is an important aspect which should be very carefully considered by the individual collector. Photographs can be vital for security and can be used to help recover stolen property. High value items such as silver and jewellery are obviously more vulnerable than others, but it is hard to believe that there are hordes of costume thieves around. For the textile collector, though, there is another aspect of photography to think about.

As mentioned previously handling items made of fabric or leather is damaging to them and photographs can help to cut this down. They can serve as an *aide-mémoire*, reminding the collector about a particular item so that it does not have to be hauled out of storage unnecessarily.

Photographs are also useful to enable an interested visitor to select which pieces she would like to take a closer look at. They are also helpful when dating garments because it is difficult to take large pieces into a reference library, possibly the only source for a particular book which will help in identifying the items.

There are a large number of cameras on the market today and they are always changing. Go to a specialist camera shop and talk to someone there who can advise on the best one for the job, at a price you are willing to pay. For photographing costume and textile items the camera must be capable of taking close-up details of things like stitches. It must also be able to take shots of mounted dresses or of very large bedspreads. Some people may want to take photographs of figures high up on cathedrals, so the camera may well need to be very versatile or have different lenses. But for those not used to a camera, or confident in using a light meter, then the simpler the better. Consider carefully the amount of auxiliary equipment necessary, such as a tripod, extra lenses and a bag for holding everything, which can all be very heavy to carry around, making travelling difficult. If the photographs are not for publication, but for helping with dating or identification, their quality is not as important as proficiency with the camera. It may not be easy to take a photograph and the quicker it can be done the simpler it may be to get permission to do it.

Instant picture cameras are not recommended for permanent records and it would be much better to spend the money on a better camera which will give permanent prints. Instant pictures can be useful for some things but it should be an additional rather than the only camera.

Apart from recording the collection for the reasons already given you must decide whether the photographs are to be used for any other purpose. Lectures on such a visual subject demand slides, while publication in articles or books needs good black and white prints. It is possible to make black and white prints from a colour slide or negative but the result will not be as clear. For reference a colour or black and white print is easier than a slide which needs to be projected. Monochrome is cheaper than colour but does not, of course, give the colours of the garment which may be important, although it often gives better definition on details. It can be very difficult to get the right colour value of the original piece on a colour film without the right lighting, and this can be a great problem if work has to be done in museum stores or other places where light is low.

It is not necessary to mount a garment on a stand or figure for photography, especially if it is a record shot. Details of embroidery, fabric and trimmings should also be taken, as well as the inside of a bodice, the boning, or dressmaker's label, if they are interesting. Hats and bonnets can be very difficult to do because they often need a head shape underneath. Shoes, if in pairs, can be photographed so that one faces forward and the other shows a side view. Some of the most difficult pieces to do are the Paisley shawls of plaid size, that is about 5 ft 9 in. by 11 ft. These usually have patterns which are duplicated in reverse on each half of the shawl with one quarter being the actual pattern, so that the size of design to take is about 2 ft 4 in. by 5 ft 9 in. However, the full magnificence of the design is not seen or appreciated unless the whole shawl is photographed. This can be done either by hanging it on a wall or on a slightly sloping board. It is a good idea to have one or two pieces of cloth which can act as backgrounds, especially for small pieces. A dark one and a light one should suffice for most occasions.

Trial and error is really the only way to find out what works best for each type of object. A good book on photography may be helpful, but there does not appear to be one written for the antique collector who merely wishes to take record shots.

CHAPTER SEVEN

Dating and identification

Dating costume is not always easy. Rarely, if ever, will it be possible to find a contemporary illustration which coincides exactly with an item in your collection. Sometimes a dress has a date, like a wedding dress or a piece of underwear with the date written on it in ink. Usually, though, dating is a question of looking at details and pin-pointing a range of dates within which a particular piece may have been made and worn. This is generally written as 'about 1840–45' or 'circa (c.) 1840–45'.

Changes in the names of items of costume are also confusing. What today is generally called a 'dress' has been a 'frock', a 'gown', a 'robe', to give only the more general terms used, not to mention a whole range of exotic names given to a particular type of dress. 'Coat' referred to the petticoat in the eighteenth century, whereas today it is an outdoor garment. So do not try to give the exotic name for any piece unless it is obvious, stick to general terms and ones that are understood today. Thus any main indoor garment for a woman can be called a dress; its date will help anyone else who knows costume to supply its original name if known.

If you have no idea of the date of a piece then the best way to start is by looking at the general shape. A one-piece dress which appears complete and is full length will probably belong to the period from about 1790 to about 1860, or the late 1870s to the early 1880s, or the period from about 1907 to 1920, when one-piece dresses were commoner. A separate bodice and skirt is usual for the periods in between. A dress with the front cut away and elbow-length sleeves is likely to be eighteenth century.

Skirts were narrow in the period from about 1790 to 1820 and got fuller after that up until the late 1860s. The 1870s and 1880s were both periods for extra pieces, such as apron fronts, separate belts and bustles at the back in various forms, as well as some very tight, sheath-like dresses. The 1890s saw the triangular-shaped skirt gradually softening to the full, floating swirl of the Edwardian era. Then skirts started to slim down again until the hobble of 1913–14, and after that they gradually began to shorten.

Waistlines were at their highest, sitting under the bust, from the period 1795 to about 1814. They then returned slowly to the natural line but often had a deep waistband which gave a slightly high-waisted look. In the 1840s to the late 1860s the waist was pointed at the front to a greater or lesser degree. It returned to normal again but, after the straight line of the late 1870s and early 1880s, became pointed in the late 1880s. The waist stayed at its normal level until the period from about 1907 to 1914 when there was a conscious return to the early nineteenth century and high waists were fashionable again.

Bodices were not generally boned until the 1840s. The heaviest

19   Detail of a bodice of the late 1830s, the one shown in the pattern, page 79. There are few pieces and the seams on the back are picked out in contrasting piping. There is one large dart at the front on each side. The bodice is open down the back and fastened by brass hooks and eyes. The skirt is cartridge pleated to the waistband at the back. The bodice is lined but not boned. *Royal Scottish Museum, 1961.448*

boning, though, is found in the last quarter of the nineteenth century when bodices were 'constructed'. In the early years of this century they acquired a very full-bosomed look, drooping over the waist and making even young girls look like middle-aged matrons.

These are not invariable rules but give guidance for where to start looking when dating women's clothes. For men it is much more difficult because there were relatively few changes by comparison and there are not so many surviving examples. A useful résumé of points to look for is found in the beginning of C. W. & P. Cunnington's *Handbook of English Costume in the Nineteenth Century* (rev. ed. 1970).

The dressmaking technique and cut of a dress are important for dating purposes. There were, for example, certain typical bodice patterns at any one time. Inside, boning will be found in the same places giving the shaping which the style of the period required. The number and shape of bodice pieces is also revealing and a look at the flat pattern can be a help. Some periods had completely lined

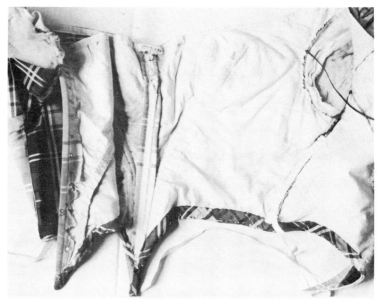

20   An evening bodice of the late 1850s to early 1860s. This has the typical longboned, pointed front and back at the waist, which must have dug into the abdomen rather painfully. There are soft pads between the armhole and the bust to fill the ugly gap which is left with a low-necked dress. *Royal Scottish Museum, 1977.156*

bodices, whereas in others the lining was more a foundation for the attachment of the bodice. Sometimes the lining was sewn so that the dress seams were not visible, in others the lining and dress material were treated as one layer.

Skirts were sometimes made up from straight widths of material and at other times there were triangular gores to give more shape without bulk at the waist. Cartridge pleating, a form of gathering, was used to compress a large amount of skirt material into the waist seam without looking too lumpy, and at other times there was only a little gathering, or unpressed pleats. The 1890s and early 1900s were a period of great innovation in the way skirts were cut and this is important for dating. The very fluid line of skirts of the 1900s was

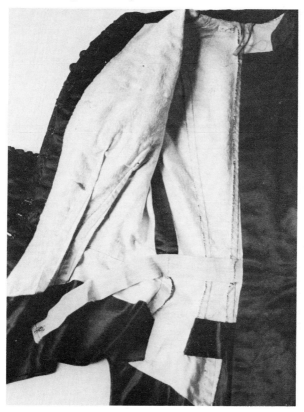

21   The long seams found on the princess line and other long bodices of the 1870s and 1880s. There are more pieces to the bodice to achieve the tight fit fashion demanded and the front edge is curved to fit over the full bosom. *Royal Scottish Museum, 1963.247*

dependent on the cut of the material and the right lining where the actual fabric was very light in weight.

Skirts were not normally lined until the fuller fashions of the mid-nineteenth century, although some very high quality silk mantua petticoats are found lined. The heavy lining in pre-cage skirts of the Victorian period helped to make them stand out and reduced the number of petticoats needed. It also added warmth for winter dresses; light summer materials were not lined. In the 1880s the lining became the skirt's foundation with the often asymmetrical drapery being sewn to the lining.

Although the sewing machine was invented in the 1840s dresses were not generally machine-sewn until the late 1850s. Even later than this some skirts had hand-sewn seams. This job was often put out to out-workers, many of whom were paid very low wages for the work and could not afford a sewing machine, although the long seams of a skirt were most suited to machine sewing. Two kinds of machine stitching were used, chain stitch and lock stitch. The former looks like a row of loops of thread and when a stitch breaks it unravels quickly, while lock stitch is the same as modern machine stitching. Sometimes both types are found together on the same dress indicating an alteration or that the dress had been made up by more than one person, which was not uncommon in large dressmaking establishments.

In the eighteenth century many seams were sewn with strong linen thread, although silk would be used for those stitches which showed. The usual stitch in skirt seams was a running stitch which was quite adequate because there was little strain on them. Bodice seams were usually done in back stitch which took the strain better. The same was true in the nineteenth century for hand-sewn dresses. Fine sewing is found on the delicate muslins and cottons of the early 1800s, while later in the century dresses from very expensive establishments can have badly matched silk and hurried sewing in the parts that do not show. This must be a legacy from the extreme haste with which some dresses had to be made.

Later in the nineteenth century and in the years up to 1914 there is some particularly fine inside finishing to be found in dresses made by the leading dressmakers. This can be seen in the detailing of the lining with hand-sewn oversewing of seams and a multiplicity of tiny fastenings to keep the various layers in place. This is a great contrast to the almost complete lack of fastenings on eighteenth-century dresses. Then they were held together by pins, although the

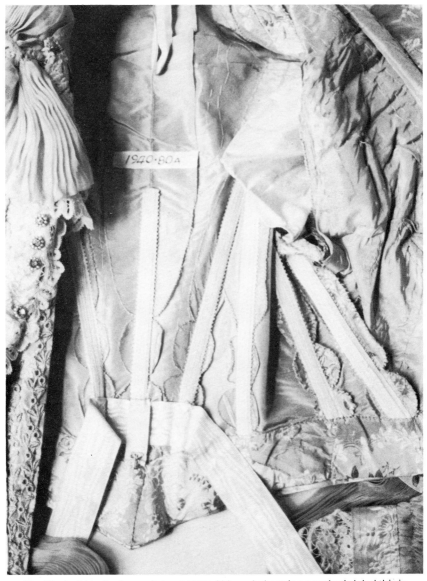

22   The inside of a dress of about 1902. Although there is no maker's label this is very high quality dressmaking. The bones are covered by fine picot-edged ribbon and the seams are oversewn by hand. The hook at the centre back of the waist is to fasten bodice and skirt together. *Royal Scottish Museum, 1940.80A*

petticoat might have ribbon ties at the waist. Drawstrings, ribbon ties and buttons are the usual fastenings for the late eighteenth and early nineteenth centuries. Flat brass hooks and eyes are found in the 1820s and from then onwards they feature as fastenings in women's dress, although they were japanned later on.

There are a whole series of ingenious fastenings invented in the nineteenth century. One which is often used in dress skirts is Nicholl's hook which was patented in 1858 and is always marked, though not usually found until about twenty years later. Another one, dating from about the same period, consists of two strips of sheet metal, one with hooks on it, the other with eyes. This would make it simpler and quicker to put fastenings onto dresses at a time when between ten and twenty hooks might be needed.

Other aids to help the dressmaker cut down on the time taken to make a dress include factory-made frills for skirt hems. These white muslin, lace-trimmed, knife-pleated frills, known as balayeuses, were worn with trained skirts from the mid-1870s to stop dirt getting onto the dress skirt. They were removed for washing and so are

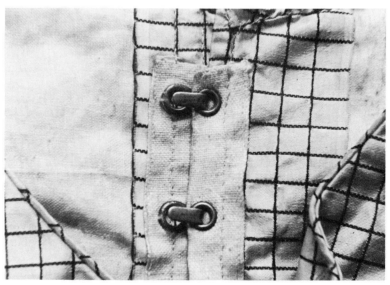

23 Detail of the fastenings on a bodice of about 1840–5. The hooks and eyes are set at regular intervals of 5/8 in. along a white tape. These tapes could obviously be bought by the yard and sewn to the bodice, which would cut down on the time needed to sew on several hooks and eyes (this bodice has fifteen). Presumably this was a patented design but the date has not yet been established. *Royal Scottish Museum, Shambellie 1629*

generally only tacked into the skirt hem. The vast amount needed must have been a tedious chore for a dressmaker to do by hand.

There is as yet no book on the history of dressmaking or tailoring techniques. This is regrettable as the changes in the details of stitching and fastenings can help to determine dates and highlight any alterations which might have been done to the garment. For men's clothes it is sometimes only in the subtle differences in the tailoring techniques that can help with dating.

PICTORIAL SOURCES

Once a garment has been thoroughly investigated inside and out-side for all the clues to its date, the collector will then have to start searching the pictorial sources to see if anything comparable can be found. Apart from books, which are dealt with separately, there are other useful aids, such as fashion plates and paintings.

Some museums issue postcards of dresses in their collections and these can be helpful. The main difficulty is finding out what is available as there is no central list of these items, and once out of print they are not often reprinted. Some commercial publishers have reprinted fashion plates, and to the costume collector these are just as useful as the original prints, at a fraction of the price.

Paintings in major art galleries are also available as postcards, although the galleries have an unfortunate habit of not putting the date of the painting on the card unless it is inscribed on the picture. This is very unhelpful for the costume collector. Paintings, as evidence, need to be used with caution as some artists used the same clothes again and again in paintings and portraits, Tissot being a notable case. But some portraits are so evocative that their correct-ness is not questioned; Zoffany's Mrs Oswald of Auchincruive in the National Gallery, London, for example. Collecting postcards and books with the work of portrait painters in them is important so that any re-use of garments can be seen. This makes it easier for you to judge whether an artist is a reliable portrayer of dress. Remember, though, that a person having their portrait painted would not want to look out of date or badly or unfashionably dressed, so the re-use of a dress in a portrait does not necessarily rule it out as evidence. However, a painter like Tissot, who was painting social scenes, had no need to be worried about using a dress two or three years out of fashion. It is only today, when we are using his work as an authority on dress in the 1870s, that we must be aware that the same pink muslin turns up in at least three well-known paintings of different dates which are often reproduced in costume books.

Photographs are another good pictorial source. There are now several books which reproduce old photographs, often showing people in informal poses and giving a better idea of more typical wear than the fashion plates. Although studio work can be enhanced and touched up it is very valuable evidence all the same. For instance, waists were often altered to make them look much smaller; even Queen Alexandra's portraits are not immune from this minor vanity. The more artistic photographers' work, such as that of Julia Margaret Cameron, is not always as good, but the numerous *cartes de visite* are much more revealing for the costume historian.

Collecting all the various types of pictorial evidence into a manageable form is helpful. Postcards are nearly always in standard sizes so pose no problem and can be stored in date order in a shoe box or filing cabinet. Fashion plates, though, come in all shapes and sizes and need to be carefully stored as they have a monetary value in their own right. To focus on such things as handbags, fans or hats it is quite sensible to photocopy a plate or postcard and cut out the detail. This can then be stuck onto plain paper, several on one sheet, in date order and kept in a file or folder. It is much easier to see an accessory when it is isolated like this, rather than having to go through a great many useless plates or postcards to find the right ones. All the information regarding which plate or painting the detail comes from should be written on it.

FASHION MAGAZINES AND PLATES

The most obvious sources to use for identifying and dating costume are the fashion plates and magazines of the past. This is an impractical suggestion for the average collector because the plates are now collected in their own right and are very expensive. Magazines also take up rather a lot of room in comparison to their usefulness, which is why the two books by Mrs Blum mentioned later on page 97 are so useful.

Complete runs of magazines in British libraries are scarce. They usually have to be used in the reference section which means that you cannot take them home for comparison with items of costume. Some museums have good fashion plate collections but few have good runs of magazines.

Fashion was first reported and illustrated in magazines in the late eighteenth century, but the remaining works are nearly all from the nineteenth and twentieth centuries. The survival of magazines depends to some extent on the number produced at the time and as there was a stamp duty on paper until 1854 this undoubtedly limited the print run. The earliest which is found in any number today is probably *La Belle Assemblée*, first issued in 1806.

But the magazine surviving in the greatest numbers is *The English-woman's Domestic Magazine*, which was produced in three series. The first one, in the 1850s, was illustrated by line drawings and included flat patterns. The second series, in the early 1860s, contained the famous colour plates by Jules David and these volumes are the most prevalent. The third series was larger in format than the second and continued with fashion plates, but also had many line drawings in the text and a lively correspondence column. The first and third

24   A fashion plate of 1862 by Jules David for a French magazine and bought by Samuel Beeton to use in the *Englishwoman's Domestic Magazine*, 2nd series, which he edited.

series are rarer but in many ways much more interesting and informative for the costume historian than the second.

Another middle-class magazine surviving in fair numbers is the *Girl's Own Paper*. It was first produced in 1880 as a weekly paper for the wives and daughters of the lower middle class, always giving good advice on how to use small dress allowances to best advantage and on the refurbishing of out-of-date clothes. It had a monthly dress article illustrated by line drawings which bear a closer resemblance to most surviving specimens than do the fashion plates and are therefore probably a better guide to general and provincial taste than the more prestigious periodicals.

The Queen is the oldest surviving magazine for women in Britain, and in the 1890s it had by far the best colour plates of the day, drawn by A. Sandoz. There were also line drawings of French fashions in the text, particularly those from Worth, often found repeated in *Harper's Bazar*. There were pages of dresses worn at fashionable weddings, sometimes showing trousseau gowns and often naming the dressmaker who made them, and in March and April there were

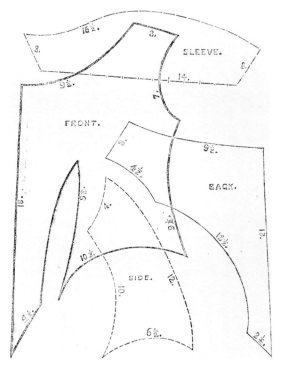

25 (above) & 26 (opposite)   A pattern and the drawing of the bodice to show what it should look like. These are from the first series of the *Englishwoman's Domestic Magazine, 1858.*

whole pages featuring Court dresses. It was an extremely large format weekly in the 1880s and 1890s and as it is usually made up in six monthly batches it weighs heavily, making it a difficult periodical to use. It does not survive in the same quantity as the earlier magazines mentioned.

After the First World War *Vogue* became the main fashion magazine, but there were by then a host of smaller and cheaper ones catering for all levels of taste and pocket. Many can be found in odd numbers today, but as the paper on which they were printed was often of inferior quality their survival rate is not high.

The twentieth century witnessed the great increase in home dressmaking and some of the pattern books such as *Weldons* or *Vogue Pattern Book* are very informative. For post-World War Two developments the couture and ready-to-wear trade magazines are probably the best sources. But magazines are cumbersome and there are too many other things in them to justify the space they take up. If you have access to a friend's collection of fashion prints or magazines, it is a good idea to photocopy or photograph the plates (copyright regulations if photocopying should be observed). These can then be filed for future use.

BOOKS FOR IDENTIFICATION

In the past museums published catalogues listing all their holdings in a specific area, and the Victoria and Albert Museum's pre-1939 catalogues are still considered to be very good. But it is now too expensive for most museums to issue this type of publication. Recent attempts in the 1960s by Worthing Museum and the Worcestershire County Museum did not have enough illustrations to make them really valuable. This is also the problem with the London Museum's (now the Museum of London) catalogues of their collection of pre-1800 clothing.

So this will be a rather small selection of books and is based on my own experience of having to catalogue quickly a large private collection. When items are catalogued in the Royal Scottish Museum there is a large library of books to call on within the building, as well as access to a copyright library with contemporary periodicals, a good public library, a university library with a fine arts department, and another museum with an excellent library of local history material. This will not be the case for the majority of collectors, nor will they have the experience that comes from daily contact with a good comprehensive collection which can be used for comparison. So, when faced with cataloguing several hundred items away from my usual sources of information and with a time limit, the books which were found to be useful were quickly reduced to a mere handful.

First came the books which show the cut of the clothes by giving the flat pattern. By far the best are the two by Janet Arnold, *Patterns of Fashion, I 1660–1860* and *II 1860–1940* (1964 and 1965 but continually reissued). Her patterns are extremely detailed and the drawings of the actual garments, mounted and completed with the relevant accessories, are very clear. Norah Waugh's two books, *The Cut of Women's Clothes 1600–1930* (Faber, 1963) and *The Cut of Men's Clothes 1600–1900* (Faber, 1964), are not as detailed as Miss Arnold's but are still very useful as she includes slightly more patterns. Her book on men's clothes is in fact the only one on the subject with patterns.

Two books, now alas long out of print, by Dr C. W. Cunnington are *Englishwomen's Clothing in the Nineteenth Century* (1937) *Englishwomen's Clothing in the Present Century* (1952). These are very detailed year by year accounts of changes in fashion taken from fashion magazines, and abundantly illustrated by good line drawings.

Covering very limited periods, but extremely useful because they are taken from original magazines, are the two books edited and selected by Stella Blum for Dover paperbacks, *Ackermans Repository 1818–1828* (1978) and *Harper's Bazar 1868–1898* (1974). The latter is an American publication and some details, such as the very handsome knickerbocker skating suits for women of 1869, were almost certainly not seen in Britain.

In the late 1940s and 1950s the Gallery of English Costume, Platt Hall, Manchester, produced a series of excellent little booklets, illustrated with garments from the collection on live models and with the correct accessories and hairstyles. These booklets were produced under Anne Buck's supervision and, because they have been dated by an expert and the people dressed with great attention to the period, they are by far the best publications of their type.

A book which many collectors will find helpful is Nancy Bradfield's *Costume in Detail* (Harrap, 1968, rev. ed. 1981). The author has drawn the insides of dresses to show their construction. It is perhaps easier for the non-dressmaker to understand than the actual patterns shown in Miss Arnold's and Miss Waugh's books. The dresses shown are nearly all the middle-class garments that are the most numerous survivors, and so reflect more closely the average costume collection. However, they lack the clarity of line which Miss Arnold's books display.

On men's clothes in the twentieth century the book by O. E. Schoeffler and William Gale, *Esquire's Encyclopedia of 20th Century Men's Fashions* (McGraw-Hill, 1973), will be useful. It is a mine of information on American men's wear this century and can be used in other countries so long as the source is borne in mind. There is often a national difference, even in fashionable wear, and an American illustration is not always going to be useful in a British context.

There are no really comparable books for children's clothing. Phillis Cunnington and Anne Buck's *Children's Costume in England* lacks the number of illustrations which would turn it into a really worthwhile book for this section.

Nor are there any very useful books on underclothes as this subject tends to attract the slightly salacious writer, but a promised updating of the Cunningtons' book on the subject may well correct this deficiency. For corsets Norah Waugh's book, *Corsets and Crinolines* (Faber, 1954), is the only one to deal with the subject recently and she gives patterns of actual garments.

These are the most useful books so far produced which will help the average collector of European fashionable dress in dating and identifying her collection. Other books may help but in comparison to their size and the subjects covered they give less value for the space they occupy on the bookshelves.

Dating a garment where the exact date is not known is really a question of arriving at a consensus from the indications that a thorough study of its cut, the dressmaking details and pictorial sources can tell. There may well be many puzzling features about a piece because an individual might have been oblivious to the current fashionable trend, the garment may belong to a rarely seen type which is not depicted in very many illustrations, or it may have belonged to an eccentric. It is very rare to find a unique type of garment and eventually, by a close study of other collections, illustrations, and by asking questions of other collectors and costume historians, the collector will find the answer. Once a new type of garment has been spotted by a collector her eye will be trained to look for that type and it is surprising how often this new awareness quickly leads to the answer. It helps too to have a memory which is good at retaining visual material.

GENERAL AND SPECIALIST BOOKS

Any collector is going to need a basic library of books on costume as well as specialist volumes. Clothing is such a part of our lives that general books on society are going to be of value too in setting a context for clothes. Clothes have an impact on all aspects of our lives. Anyone who does not believe this should study the daily newspapers where they are likely to find fashion news, a piece on the recession in the textile industry, the imports of foreign clothes, decrees against immodest dress issued by some government, and the stock market listing of firms with textiles and chemical interests.

Books on the textile industry are particularly relevant as well as social history books. People's memoirs, letters, diaries and journals are all rich costume sources which put clothes in the perspective of their own time.

The books written on costume fall into two categories; those useful for dating and identification, and those which describe the development of dress or discuss a theme. The second category, though, no matter how well illustrated, seldom have the right kind of pictures for purposes of identification.

A general history of costume is a good basic book for a collector's library. This is not an easy topic to write on because it demands compression of a complex subject which can lead to mis-statements. There is no very recent work that is thoroughly reliable and the two earlier ones noted below are probably the best so far.

The Book of Costume by Millia Davenport was first published in 1948 in two volumes and then reissued in one volume in 1972. It is a profusely illustrated history of costume from the beginning to 1870 in western Europe and America. A projected updating has not yet appeared. *A History of Costume in the West* by François Boucher was published in Britain by Thames and Hudson in 1967 and deals with European costume from the prehistoric period to 1947.

A bibliography is essential. There is an excellent one produced by the Costume Society compiled by Pegaret Anthony and Janet Arnold which lists about 400 books and articles under various headings. This is updated at intervals to take account of any new works. Much more comprehensive ones, which will only be available through specialist libraries, are: *Katalog der Freiherrlich von Lipperheid'schen Kostümbibliothek*, edited by E. Neinholdt and G. Wagner Neumann (new ed., 2 vols, Berlin 1965); *Bibliographie generale du costume et de la mode*, by R. Colas (Paris, 1933) and *Bibliography of Costume*, by H. & M. Hiler (New York, repr. 1967).

The Costume Society also publish a guide to books on *European Folk Dress*, by James Snowden. This lists about 500 books and other sources of information on the subject.

To keep up to date on new books certain journals usually list those which are relevant and recently published. They also review books. *British Book News*, published by the British Council, often reviews more costume and textile books than does the *Times Literary Supplement*, and it has a useful new books section each month. There are also specialist booksellers who, as well as selling second-hand and antiquarian, keep a range of recent new books.

A very good book which is difficult to slot into a definite category is *Handbook of Costume* by Janet Arnold, published in 1973 and regularly reprinted. It is a mine of information on sources of all kinds for the study of costume and is filled with beautiful drawings in the author's clear and elegant style. It is of great value to teachers and gives much practical advice not found elsewhere. Teachers might also find useful *Exploring Costume History 1500–1900* by Valerie Cumming (1981), which was written specifically for them and for schoolchildren who are doing costume history projects.

The Museums Association in Britain produces various leaflets which are helpful for curators, but the general costume collector may find their *Textiles: their care and protection*, by Jean Glover, of interest. These leaflets are periodically updated as they often include names and addresses of suppliers of equipment. Collectors in other countries may well find that their own museums association produces similar leaflets which they can obtain.

Specialist collecting areas, such as fans, are well supplied with their own list of books, but the general costume collector may be interested in the following: *Fans from the East* (Debrett's Peerage, the Fan Circle and the V & A, 1978); *The Book of Fans*, Nancy Armstrong (Colour Library International); *The Identification of Lace*, Pat Earnshaw (Shire Publications, 1980); *Victorian Lace*, Patricia Wardle (Herbert Jenkins, 1968); *Machine-made Lace in Nottingham in the 18th and 19th centuries*, Zillah Halls (Nottingham Museum and Art Gallery, 1964); *Shoes*, June Swann, Costume Accessories Series (Batsford, 1982); *The Shoe Show: British Shoes since 1790*, K. & K. Baynes (Crafts Council, London, 1979); *Bags and Purses*, Vanda Foster, Costume Accessories Series (Batsford, 1982); *Discovering Embroidery in the 19th century*, Santina Levey (Shire Publications, 1971).

Shire Publications have a whole series of small illustrated albums on topics such as beadwork, fashion accessories, needlework tools, samplers, shawls, and smocks, which the collector will find useful and informative introductions to these subjects. They also have one or two in their *Discovering* series, which are longer accounts but well illustrated.

Two books using photographs as their illustrations are: *Fashion and Reality 1840–1914* by Alison Gernsheim (Faber, 1963), republished as *Victorian and Edwardian Fashion in Photographs* (Dover, 1981) and *David Octavius Hill and Robert Adamson* by Sara Stevenson (National Galleries of Scotland, 1981). The former is a study of fashion from the start of photography to 1914, showing how the camera illustrated the clothes. The latter is a complete catalogue of the Scottish National Portrait Gallery's holdings of Hill and Adamson photographs. This is probably the largest collection in the world and numbers over 2,000 dated between 1843 and 1846 and, with each one being illustrated, it makes a fascinating source for the costume historian.

Two books which costume enthusiasts might enjoy reading are the autobiographies of two collectors, describing how they built up their collections. *Looking over my Shoulder* is by C. W. Cunnington, the well-known costume historian. It was published in 1961 shortly after his death and is little known. The other is by Charles W. Stewart, who gave his collection to the Royal Scottish Museum. It is now displayed in his old family home at Shambellie House Museum of Costume near Dumfries. The book, *Holy Greed; the forming of a collection* (Royal Scottish Museum, 1982), is illustrated with some of Mr Stewart's delightful drawings of his collection.

C. W. Cunnington is one of the major costume historians and he wrote many books on the subject, sometimes with his wife, Phillis, as co-author. The main ones used today are the series of *Handbooks on English Costume* from the Middle Ages to the present. These are very helpful sources for general trends in fashion but are often less useful for dating as they lack the number of illustrations needed to cover so wide a topic. He also wrote on the psychology of clothing including *The Perfect Lady*, *Why Women Wear Clothes*, and *Feminine Attitudes in the Nineteenth Century*. Another author who wrote on this topic was James Laver. His best known book is probably *Taste and Fashion*.

Three books by Anne Buck, who was for many years Keeper of the Gallery of English Costume, must be mentioned for their scholarship and readability. They are not meant primarily for identification but are general essays on the subject and are very good background reading for any collector. These are: *Victorian Costume and Costume Accessories* (1961), *Children's Costume in England 1300–1900*, with Phillis Cunnington (1965), and *Dress in Eighteenth Century England* (1979).

On the whole, recent writers have left the pre-1900 period alone but there has been a deluge of books on the twentieth century. Most of these are useless for dating and identification purposes, dominated as they are by French haute couture and the leading members of this circle just before and after the First World War. These books overemphasise the importance of Paris and take at its face value the fashion journalism of the time. Nevertheless, some of these books will be useful because there are always some photographs which are relevant.

One particular book published recently, *A Fashion Parade: The Seeburger Collection* by Celestine Dars (1979), shows photographs of the clothes being worn out of doors. Most of the people are either rich or mannequins but it is heartening to see that even they did not always dress according to the current fashion rules, and it is an interesting contrast to some of the books illustrated exclusively by the elegant colour plates from *Gazette du Bon Ton* and its rivals.

On individual couturiers Diana de Marly's book, *Worth, the Father of Haute Couture* (1980), is a detailed look at the first great name of Paris fashion who dressed the Empress Eugenie and who was British. Mariano Fortuny, a rather eccentric designer who was very well liked by a certain circle of European and American women in the 1920s and 1930s, has been dealt with in several books published recently.

The most difficult type of book, but sometimes the most useful for a collector to have, is an exhibition catalogue. Many museums have no outlet for their publications except their own bookstall and, because there are no trade outlets, information on them can be difficult to obtain. They are rarely reviewed in the press and invariably go out of print quite quickly. The Costume Society tries to cover these each year in its journal but there is no really comprehensive list.

Some museums have published excellent detailed studies of areas which would not be commercially viable for a trade publisher. These include two produced recently: *Madame Clapham, the Celebrated Dressmaker* by Ann Crowther (Kingston upon Hull Museum, 1976), and *Liverpool Fashion its Makers and Wearers: the Dressmaking Trade in Liverpool, 1830–1940* by Anthea Jarvis (Merseyside County Museum, 1981). Both these are very good detailed studies of a little researched area.

This is by no means an exhaustive list of books but it tries to give some idea of the published work on costume. Recently several series of books on costume were announced indicating the awareness of the publishing trade of the great general interest in the subject. But whether this will produce the kind of books the collector and curator need for dating and identifying costume pieces is doubtful. So the collector must still be prepared to make her own archive for this task.

CHAPTER EIGHT

Displays and exhibitions

PRACTICALITIES OF EXHIBITION WORK

Display work is the 'fun' part of collecting but, as anyone who has done it will know, it is not as easy as it looks. Before taking on an exhibition the collector should find out (or be told, if she is lending) where the items are to be shown and for how long, how much time there will be for mounting the display, and who will be paying for display aids and catalogues. Another important consideration is insurance, and this must be sorted out in the early stages. On no account should you agree to do an exhibition unless your own insurance policy, or one taken out by the organisers, covers damage to items on display. There will always be some damage and even if it can be mended easily, the organisers should be made aware of the personal and intrinsic value attached to the exhibits.

Once these points are settled there are more practical aspects to consider. Do you have enough items for the space available, can they be attractively displayed, and will there be enough space for people to circulate round them? In addition you may want to supplement your material by borrowing from friends.

The organisers of any exhibition should give plenty of advance notice of the date and of their intentions. If this is not satisfactory you should say so. A lot of hard work goes into the smallest costume display and exhibitors need time to do justice to their pieces. If the display is to be fairly large, involving several figures, then make a different person responsible for a specific topic, like wigs or setting up a particular figure. Avoid committees and just work with a group of people you know.

The next step is to assemble all the garments and see that they are in a good enough condition to withstand display. Do any repair work, such as sewing on buttons, and examine all the pieces, noting their condition so that they can be checked for damage after the exhibition. Every item should be catalogued and bear the owner's name, and this is a good time to photograph them if it has not been done already.

Put together and list all the pieces which will be used on one figure, making sure that they complement each other in date and appearance. This will highlight any items needed to complete the outfit, such as collars or a flower spray for the hair.

If the items for display are small and to be shown in cases, then measure the cases inside and make sure that they lock. The area of each case can be marked out on graph paper to scale, or roughly indicated on the floor, and the pieces arranged for maximum effect. You could make a rough sketch of where each piece is to go so that the actual positioning of them can be done quickly on the day.

Labels and Handlists
Labels or a duplicated handlist of the items are a must. For labels black type on white is by far the easiest to read, and they must be fairly large if they are to go on the floor beside the exhibits. For a display in the rooms of a house, labels might be too obtrusive, so a handlist would be better with numbers put beside the figures, or a sketch plan done of the group.

The information on the labels should be fairly succinct, as reading them might cause a bottleneck in the flow of visitors, but do give more than just 'Dress, 1815'. The fabric of the garments, the date of the piece, its name, who made it and who wore it is the kind of information that helps to make costume more alive. Further details can go into a handlist or small booklet, but it is a good idea to work out a set pattern so that the labels or handlist look neat. For example:

> DRESS of white muslin embroidered in white cotton.
> British, about 1815.
> Belonged to Mrs Anne Smith, 1790–1840.
> Lent by Mrs G. Smith.

If the labels are being typed then a good clear typeface is necessary, and use a carbon ribbon so that the type is a good black – they can also be done with instant letters, such as Letraset. If the labels are to be handwritten then do them in clear, easy-to-read handwriting, such as a calligraphic or copperplate script. Presentation details are so important even for a one-day event and make an exhibition look that little bit more professional and attractive.

Design and Lighting

Good background design is an important consideration and should never obtrude and impair the visitors' enjoyment of the objects. The overall effect must be considered, and as this can be an expensive exercise think carefully how to do it. A friend who is a designer or window dresser may well be able to give some advice but if in doubt, keep things simple. A well-arranged flower display can do a lot more to make a room attractive than having elaborate drapes and period effects. If the displays are in a house then some of the family clutter, such as modern photographs, might be removed in case they detract from the costumes.

Lighting is important both for the clothes and for the visitors, and somehow the irreconcilable needs of the two have to be met. If a display is to be up for any length of time the costumes must not be put in direct sunlight or beside a window. Windows can have muslin curtains fitted so that the light is filtered and diffused. Any artificial lighting should use bulbs with low ultra-violet levels, as this is the most damaging area in the light spectrum. Powerful spotlights should be avoided at all costs. It is a good idea to reduce light levels gradually rather than to plunge visitors suddenly into a very dimly lit room, but do not forget that visitors will need some light to see their way round and to read labels.

Security Aspects

During an exhibition the organisers may well provide some kind of warding to prevent visitors touching the displays, but if this is lacking try and organise something yourself. You may wish to be present and answer questions as this type of display attracts a lot of comment, especially if clothes from the twentieth century are on exhibition. Visitors often like to comment about what they wore at that period and this can be a helpful source of information.

At the end of an exhibition equal care is needed in the dismantling. This is the time of greatest danger to the objects because it often has to be done in a shorter time than was allowed for putting the exhibition up. Use only the people who helped put up the display as they will know how a particular dress was pinned and where. Flower displays, which can be knocked over and spill water

on the clothes, should be removed first. Otherwise, purely decorative features can be left until last.

Once the hazards are out of the way remove any mounted figures
outside the cases. It is best to undress the figure on the spot as
damage can be done when they are moved fully clothed. Items in
cases can be left until later, but once a case is opened clear it
completely and do not leave it open with things in it. Insist that you
and your colleagues have the room to yourselves to put up and take
down the display, as damage can easily occur if any other activity is
going on, and make it clear that no one else must move the figures
once they have been set up.

Once back at home, inspect the items carefully and assess any
damage done and contact the organisers immediately. Do any
minor repairs before all the pieces go back into store and note on
each item's catalogue card when and where it has been displayed.
This can be a help in making sure pieces are not used too often.

If the display has been a success and the exercise an enjoyable one
then you may well want to repeat it. If so, a few notes on any points
to remember for the future are a good idea, as display work is always
made easier by experience.

Borrowing and Lending
Costume displays are often collaborative efforts of one or more
collectors but only one person should be in charge of the arrangements. However, whether you are borrowing for or lending to an
exhibition the same courteous procedures apply.

Once a collector has agreed to lend to an exhibition she should
receive details as to the place, dates, scope, security and purpose of
the event. Other questions, such as insurance during display and
transportation, together with the valuation of the items, should all
be agreed by letter; telephone calls are not enough. She, in turn,
must supply information for the labels or handlist.

If there is to be a private view then all those lending items should
be invited with their husband, wife, or friend. When it is all over
letters of thanks should be sent and, if they were not able to get to
the exhibition, it is a good idea to say how many people came to see it
and, if it was in aid of a charity, how much was raised. A photograph
of the lender's item on display may be of interest to her for her
records.

A collector lending items for display may wish to remain anonymous and should make this clear to the organisers. Otherwise she

should state how she wishes to be acknowledged – for example 'Lent by Mrs A. K. Smith'. In Britain there is a tendency to use the verb 'to loan' instead of 'to lend' when writing museum labels. 'Loaned by . . .' sounds extremely ugly when read aloud so perhaps we could return to the phrase 'Lent by . . .' for exhibition labels.

Exhibitions are usually scenes of chaos and, with so many people around, the objects are at their most vulnerable. So it is important for the lender to find out about how the piece will be displayed and who will mount it or handle it. It may be better to take the pieces over yourself to see how things are going if the people are unknown to you. It is also important to find out about the conditions of the display areas to make sure it is not dirty or too light. Look at the security, too. Will visitors be discouraged from touching everything on open display? Will the display cases be securely locked?

Most collectors are flattered to be asked to show their pieces and they can overlook things in the excitement of a display or exhibition. But no one can make you lend items from your collection and if there is anything about the proposed exhibition which you do not like, then refuse firmly but politely to lend to it. If, having agreed to lend, you find that things which were agreed are not being done, or that there are new developments which you do not like, then you are at liberty to remove your items. At all times you must consider the safety of your pieces. If the organisers are being inconsiderate or not doing as they agreed then they should be made aware of their shortcomings. Exhibitions are not easy to arrange and carry through smoothly from start to finish without a good deal of thought and planning and anyone who ignores the preliminary work has only themselves to blame if the result is a lot of upset lenders and an exhibition which is less than perfect.

MOUNTING GARMENTS FOR DISPLAY

When mounting a costume display there is always the problem of making the clothes come alive in a way that is reminiscent of their original wearers. Although certain types of garment are seen as decorative objects in their own right, most of the clothes are viewed by the public as having been worn by their ancestors, and they like to see them shown in a way that suggests there is a body underneath rather than a headless stand. A number of costume curators, however, dislike this type of figure and would like to see one that is versatile yet safe for the clothes and which does not have a twentieth century look about it. After years of investigating this problem I can foresee no solution to it unless a radical new material is discovered, which would form a pliable body but with the strength to let the figure stand when fully clothed. None of the solutions at present available is ideal, but some museums have taken the view that there is no point in waiting for the impossible and have adaped to their needs various figures which are available commercially.

Figures or Stands

Most private collectors find good display figures hard to come by and bulky to store afterwards. Second-hand models from the windows of dress shops and department stores are not usually suitable for antique clothing. Women's figures in particular often have exaggerated poses which, though suitable for current fashion, would look terrible displaying a nineteenth-century dress. Some modern men's figures are better but may be too broad in the shoulders, or too well-developed in the legs, to be usable.

However good the figure, it does not necessarily mean that a well-mounted exhibit will result. There is a good deal of skill required in making a static display figure come alive and a basic idea of the human anatomy is essential to get the right effect. Flair and imagination are useful commodities, but a good window dresser is not necessarily a good dresser of antique clothes – they demand different techniques.

Old clothes must be safely displayed. This means that figures, if used, should not fit the clothes exactly but be thinner all over so that you can achieve a perfect fit by soft padding, which will not strain the costume. Sometimes you have to cut figures at the waist or remove the modern bust to build up the correct shape.

In Britain the most realistic figures used by museums are those produced by Gems Wax Models for use in their waxworks. The bodies are made of fibreglass with wax heads and hands, but for museums these are cast in fibreglass too. The heads depict well-known people which have been modelled from life, or, in the case of historic characters, based on a portrait. These figures are very useful for permanent displays like farmhouse kitchens where the figure wears reproduction clothes, but they are also used with a degree of success for more temporary exhibitions. They are not easy to manoeuvre and when fully clothed are heavy, but with skillful handling they can be made to yield very satisfactory displays. They

27 An embroidered white cotton summer dress of about 1910 with a large straw hat and collecting tin for Alexandra Rose Day. The face is very stylised with only the main features indicated. The hair is of hemp. *Museum of London*

are expensive to buy but have a long life-expectancy. Gems figures are being used in photographs 5, 8, 9, 11, 34 and 35.

In America many museums use figures which were developed by Jerry Roe. These have realistic faces but are not based on actual people. They are slightly stylised and have a refined air about them, which is suitable for a decorative arts museum, though less effective for a mock-up of a frontiersman's log cabin.

The figures just described are both fully articulated to a certain degree so that they can be shown in slightly different positions. The most fully articulated, however, are the lay-figures which are used by artists when painting the clothes in a portrait. One collector, who owns a beautiful nineteenth-century example, has been able to put it in some very natural poses. But they have rather heavy, fixed stands with moveable legs, so they cannot show short skirts very attractively. These figures are not easy to find second-hand.

Another fairly useful source is contemporary shop models from

28   A Jerry Roe figure used to display a Court presentation dress of brocaded white satin trimmed with tulle and ostrich feathers, made in about 1885 by Mrs Stratton, 104 Piccadilly, London, for Miss Crocker to wear at the British Court. Mrs Stratton was one of the leading dressmakers of the 1880s. *Museum of the City of New York, 75.53.1a–d*

29 A photograph of Miss Harriet Valentine Crocker in the dress shown in photo 28. Although the dress has been beautifully mounted by the Museum it is impossible to achieve the upholstered look of the original wearer. She is literally soft flesh encased in steel, and what is displaced at the waist is forced upwards and downwards, creating a more rounded bosom and abdomen. *Museum of the City of New York*

the 1920s onwards. These will only be suitable for clothes of the same period, but if you are specialising in the 1920s to the present, it might be worthwhile trying to acquire some of these.

Many museums have had to use headless stands because they could not afford complete figures. Some firms, such as Siegel and Stockman in London, make period-shaped display stands which are very useful and much cheaper than figures (see photograph 17). You can buy these dressmakers' stands second-hand but they may be in a very bad state and need a good deal of renovation.

However, there are several ways of making these dress-maker-style stands which show the figure from neck to hips. Janet Arnold suggests one very good method, using chicken wire padded and covered in stockinet, in her *Handbook of Costume* (1973, p. 135 with good drawings). This stand also has arms which can be attached to the framework. Norwich Museum has developed a method of copying a dress stand by using strips of gummed paper over a cotton jersey base. This is very cheap and can be used to take a cast from a person, and so long as the framework is strengthened afterwards to take the weight of clothing it is a fairly sturdy stand. All these stands have adjustable poles for the height.

Another idea is to cut a shape from plywood which gives a basic shoulder-line extending to the waist and tapering slightly. It can then be padded out to a body shape using the plywood as a firm basis for anchoring the wadding. Stockinet or cloth over this gives a smooth skin to the stand, and the neck can be made from card covered in fabric and sewn to the body shape. The plywood frame is attached to an adjustable stand by being bolted between two pieces of wood at the top, but remember to fix the height first before the padding is done. If you have a storage problem the plywood bases can be removed from the stands and stored flat.

An adaptation of this is to use a wooden coat-hanger as the shoulder-line base. These methods are both suitable for light dresses, but a heavy bustle dress of the 1880s for example might need a firmer dress stand to take the weight of the material and give a good shape to the back. Modern dressmaking stands, or those made of wickerwork, must be covered with some suitable fabric first so that any protruding parts do not snag the clothes.

In some museums when the cases have been too narrow to take a fully mounted figure, other devices have had to be used. A flat plywood, or softboard, outline of the body covered in felt or some other material can be quite effective. The dress needs to be lightly padded at the waist, bust and hips, but the rest of it can be carefully folded behind the outline. This method was used at the Victoria and Albert Museum in part of their costume display in the 1960s and 1970s. The Museum of Costume at Bath has also used it against backgrounds of painted scenes, and Worthing Museum has shown children's clothes most effectively this way by turning the outlines into silhouettes. Although this is a particularly good idea for temporary exhibitions it has dangers for more permanent displays, because the bunched up material at the back can be damaged by heavy creasing and folding.

At the Royal Scottish Museum, where the old cases were only about nine inches deep but very high, we did things slightly differently. Many of the pieces were mounted on soft body shapes and hung from the top of the cases at the right height. Hats, wigs or head-dresses were also suspended at the correct height and shoes

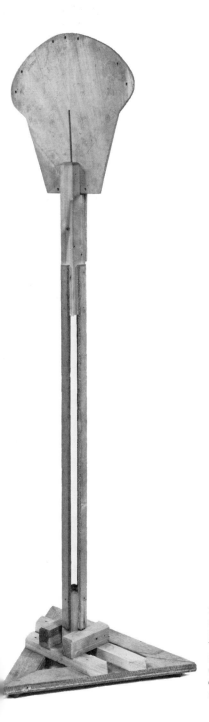

30 (*Left*) The stand used under photo 31 and described on page 112. The top piece is of plywood cut to give a shoulder line. This can be mounted on a fixed stand, as here, or on an adjustable stand. It was also used for the basis of the hanging figures described on page 112. *Royal Scottish Museum*

31 (*Above*) White cotton dress of about 1800–5. It is mounted on the stand shown in photo 30, which has been covered in soft wadding and flesh-coloured fabric. This dress illustrates the problems of mounting clothes dating from the early nineteenth century where there is no bodice shape to help with the padding. *Royal Scottish Museum, 1975.5*

were put in the bottom of the case. Some animation was attempted by putting the sleeves and legs in suitable positions. Strong nylon fishing line was used so that the means of suspension was not too obvious to the visitor.

Worthing Museum has used an ingenious way of putting heads on headless stands. The heads are of polystyrene which are used for storing wigs. Painted with make-up crayons and then covered with some light beige nylon tights they look very effective from a dis-

32 Two figures wearing dresses from about 1828. Their heads are made of polystyrene and are generally used for wigs. The features have been put in by make-up crayons and the heads have been covered in nylon tights, which are also used to make the hair. This pair have the stylised formality of a fashion plate of the period. The display was done with little money and shows what imaginative design and good mounting of the costumes can achieve. *Worthing Museum and Art Gallery*

tance, but rather crude when viewed close to. Marrying up heads and bodies is fine but it has dangers when used with low-necked dresses as a very ugly join line can result.

Dressing a Figure

Whichever method you choose there are certain points to remember. If a hard material figure is being used, such as fibreglass or plaster, then some kind of body covering is necessary to protect the costumes. The material needs to be stable so that the dye or bleach does not leach out onto the clothes. The coverings can also hold any extra padding which is needed, and if a fluffy-surfaced wadding is being used then they stop it sticking to the garments. The covering does not have to be flesh-coloured but could be any shade which enhances the dress being shown.

Any pins used should be white brass ones and not steel which will rust if there is any moisture around, and this will make them difficult to extract from the clothes, possibly leaving small rust spots which are so hard to remove.

When mounting dresses it is crucial to get the hemline at the correct height. Too often, dresses are shown trailing on the ground when they should come only to the level of the instep. The lack of shoes under a long dress is not really noticeable if the figure is standing at the same ground level as the visitor. In Victorian photographs the feet were often removed, so to have the dress floating without lower limbs is not against the spirit of the age.

The stance of the figure is very important. A straight back was

33 Cut velvet dress by Worth, worn with a Court train of Brussels application lace, about 1911. This figure illustrates two problems. The original wearer was 6ft tall but the fibreglass model was only 5½ft. Some height was achieved at the waist by an inset tube but six extra inches made it unstable, so her dress had to trail slightly. There is also a wide gap between the figure's bosom and that of the dress. Fortunately, being so tall and on a raised dais, the neckline was above the viewer's eye level. *Royal Scottish Museum, 1970.1034*

considered necessary for both men and women until the First World War, so the sloppy posture of modern shop figures is totally wrong for antique clothes.

The bustline is another area which can cause problems. You will find that early nineteenth-century dresses with very high bustlines, but without bones inside them, are very difficult to mount. The tightly boned bodices of the 1840s are much easier because if the padding follows the shape of the bodice then the correct figure will result. Be extra careful when padding very low-necked dresses because, if the figure is much smaller than the dress, there could be a very ugly gap between the neck edge of the dress and the figure.

When tight lacing was in vogue the flesh displaced had to go somewhere else and so women tended to have fuller bosoms and

34 Wedding dress of about 1925. The dress was made for a tall, large woman. Off the figure it looked very unattractive but when it was mounted the solid shape of the fibre-glass figure provided the correct curves of the body and the dress 'came alive'. *Royal Scottish Museum, 1965.634*

more rounded abdomens and hips. It was not fashionable to have a flat stomach or narrow hips and this is often forgotten when mounting up a figure. Another danger is to forget that during the years when straight fashions were in, – the early nineteenth century and from 1910 to 1930 – women had normal figures with busts, waists and hips. A look at contemporary photographs will often reveal that even in the late 1920s most women did not manage to do away with their curves.

In the eighteenth century side hoops were worn sitting on the hips, not at the waist. They would have been almost unwearable if hung from the waist, but moving them to the hips allowed them to sit lower down and let the arms move more easily. The nineteenth-century crinoline frames were on waistbands but they were not as cumbersome as the earlier hoops, since lighter materials were used and they did not usually start until hip level.

When mounting dresses which need a framework of hoops it may be easier to make one rather than use an authentic one. For the eighteenth-century variety you can either use a pattern taken from an original, like those shown in Norah Waugh's book, *Corsets and Crinolines*, or be ingenious and use other materials. The frame supporting the Court mantua in photos 11 & 35 was made from two poles to give the right width at the top. These were covered with brown paper to give the outline shape and a piece of flexible plastic was fastened round the bottom to hold out the hem. Tissue paper was used to soften the top and to prevent the acid in the brown paper from getting onto the fabric. This was an exceptionally wide dress, being five feet from side to side at the hem, and there were no suitable examples to hand for copying a proper hoop. Also, as the dress was to be on display for at least a year, the hoop had to be fairly firm to withstand the weight for that length of time.

Apart from padding the figure to get the correct body shape, the skirts of most dresses will need some kind of support. Even the flimsy ones of the early nineteenth century were usually worn over a corset and petticoat, whatever the more prurient caricaturists of the time would have us believe. Nearly all underwear at this period was made of white linen, the fineness depending on the wealth of the wearer. The basic set of undergarments worn by a respectable woman would have consisted of a chemise to the knees with short sleeves, a corset from bust to hips, and at least one full-length petticoat covering the corset and reaching to within an inch or so of the dress hem. A little roll might have been worn in the small of the

35   Court dress, about 1760. This is the front of the mantua seen in photo 11. It is
an unaltered specimen which is rare. The skirts are held out by the framework
described on page 118. The stomacher is a reconstruction. The bust is too low on
this figure but the dress was shown from the back as this was more interesting.
The arms are jointed at the elbow. The leading foot has a shoe made for it as there
were none in the collection which fitted. *Royal Scottish Museum, 1977.241&A*

36 Underwear from about 1825–35 showing what was worn under a dress like photo 37, and therefore what gave it its shape. The sleeve puffs held out the large sleeves, whilst the stiffened frills at the back helped to give fullness to the skirt. Cords in the bottom of the petticoat held out the hem. Access to the pocket was through slits in the side seams. *The Gallery of English Costume, Platt Hall, Manchester*

back to prevent the fullness of the dress from clinging to the figure. White stockings gartered above the knee would have completed her underclothes. Drawers were not commonly worn until mid-century. Winter and age might have meant that more than one petticoat was worn, or that flannel ones and a flannel waistcoat would be added. These minimal garments would still have given a fairly firm base to a dress even in 1800.

The fuller the skirt the greater the number of petticoats used, and for the pre-cage period in the 1850s as many as five or six were worn. However, there is a danger of putting too many petticoats underneath. Some people wore their dresses fuller than others, so the actual garment should be allowed to 'tell' the person mounting it how many it needs, taking into account that heavy wool or silk will press down on the petticoats and flatten them. The hem must not be uneven. In the 1850s bodices had very long, pointed fronts so the petticoats were on yokes cut to fit the hips. When using fashion

37 Muslin day dress of about 1828–30 which would have been worn over underwear similar to that shown in photo 36. *The Gallery of English Costume, Platt Hall, Manchester*

plates or photographs to help in mounting a dress it is as well to remember that both can be showing an ideal; quite often the camera was made to lie.

Crinolines are easy to make using modern flexible boning, but it is an idea to follow an original to get the placing of the boning right. There were a bewildering variety of hoops to suit every new fashion, and later on bustles were equally varied. Brown paper is a very good substitute provided it is new and of a heavy quality. It can be quickly and easily pinned to shape and, with a light cotton cover over it to stop any acids getting on the clothes, it does away with the need to have a lot of petticoats. This can make the mounted figure lighter to move too. Brown paper is an excellent base for any skirt shape.

For heavy padding wadding is much better than crumpled-up tissue paper as it will give a softer outline and be firmer. Terylene wadding is good but may be expensive. The most popular one in Britain today is of cotton, known as greyskin wadding, and is normally used for upholstery. Foam rubber must be avoided, as should any non-inert synthetics, because they may break down into unpleasant chemicals. If you are in doubt about wadding cover it with acid-free tissue paper or unbleached calico.

Mounting men's clothes can be more difficult because they need to have legs. A breeches outfit can create particular problems as a good leg shape from knee to ankle has to be produced. Eighteenth-century breeches hung from the hips but were tight fitting to the

38   A Court suit of about 18
as worn by officials. Similar
photo 5. This shows a man's s
mounted on a figure withc
head and hands. The arms a
merely wires padded to shap
Royal   Scottish   Museu
1914.327

thigh in the latter part of the century. As coats were cut away at the front and waistcoats ended at the waist breeches were very much on show, whereas in the first half of the century they were covered by the long, full-skirted coats and waistcoats.

Trousers are easier to mount because the legs underneath only need to be wooden sticks padded up to give a correct leg shape. As with women's dresses do not forget that under the tube of the trouser leg men have a shape with thighs, knees, calves and ankles. Men's coat sleeves just need to be padded to give an arm shape underneath, possibly over a wire framework.

T-shaped garments, such as kimonos, can be displayed on T-shaped frames. A dowelling pole across the top of a stand with the arms well padded will show this type of item to advantage. It is also useful for leather pieces where the material has become rather stiff and could be damaged by more realistic mounting.

Shoes are a general problem as most types of display figure have a spike through one foot which drops into a metal stand. This firm anchorage is necessary for the model to stand upright without danger of falling over. Do not use original shoes as a hole has to be cut in one of them to get it on the figure, and the hard foot may well damage an old shoe if it is forced on. For some periods, such as the last fifty years, enough shoes of indifferent quality exist for a collector to amass plenty for display figures if they are going to do a lot of this type of work.

Very scruffy shoes can be recovered or painted, but cutting a hole in the sole is not easy, especially if they have a steel spring as in modern high heels.

Certain types of shoe can be hired from theatrical costumiers or bought from dance shops, but for something like an eighteenth-century shoe other means have to be found. Where the dress is short enough to expose the whole foot then you should try and provide at least one realistic shoe. A vamp (the top of the shoe) can always be cut from suitable fabric or leather but getting the sole right is more difficult. Heels can be carved out of polystyrene and covered with fabric or leather. Original shoes could be placed beside the figure so that it is easier for the viewer to see them than if they were under the dress.

Hair can be imitated in several different ways. Recent displays have made use of coloured tissue paper over a papier-mâché or newspaper base, coloured knitting wools and tow. Nylon tights or stockings can be effective and very cheap as old laddered ones can be used. Some nylon wigs are too difficult to arrange in elaborate hairstyles but are suitable for simple ones – real hair wigs being very expensive. It may be possible to hire wigs from a theatrical costumier if the display is to last for a very short time.

Hands can create some problems too. If there are no hands on the figure then stuffed gloves are often used, but these need to be very carefully done or they can look like a bunch of sausages. Women wore gloves most of the time in the nineteenth century, even indoors, and they are one of the most useful ways of dealing with the hand problem. The smallness of unused kid gloves can deceive, so do remember that most women bought gloves a size smaller than their hands and then had to squeeze them on. Therefore, gloves should always look as if they are fitting very tightly.

Flat textiles and Small Items

The simplest method of display is to put the garments flat against a wall or hang them up on a coat-hanger without any body support inside. If the display is to last merely a day then this is certainly the quickest method and possibly the cheapest. The wall or board for supporting the clothes must be clean and covered with material which will not be harmful to the pieces.

It is not a good idea to stick pins through the garments as the sole means of hanging them up, in case the suspended weight tears holes in the fabric. Better to pass tapes through the arms from side to side with enough left at each end so that the pins can go through these instead. Alternatively, tapes can be sewn to the clothes, but see that they are attached at strong points and not to delicate areas, and use enough to support the garment properly so that the weight is evenly distributed. The pins used should be white brass and they come in several sizes suitable for most weights. This hanging method of display should not really be done for any length of time.

Pinning is suitable for smaller pieces such as embroidery or lace, again provided the pins will hold the weight. A better way is to mount the exhibit on net or calico, which is larger in size, and then stick pins through this backing. If desk cases are used no pinning is needed.

For more permanent display, or for keeping really delicate pieces flat, then framing is probably the best method. The piece should be mounted on a backing of natural linen, silk or calico which is cut to a larger size. Then stretch the backing gently over a hardboard base, turn the edges over and secure them by glueing with a PVA wood glue or sewing. A window mount will be needed, cut from acid-free board or conservation card. The window must be large enough to show the textile and the card deep enough so that when the piece is glazed the glass rests on the card mount, not on any part of the textile. The mounted piece can then be framed and glazed in the ordinary way. The back should be sealed to keep out the dust.

It is now fairly common to hang large textiles, even tapestries, by Velcro. This is bought in two parts by the yard or metre. The length which is sewn to the hanging is a kind of soft plush, while the part that is attached to a wooden batten, or board, is composed of thousands of tiny hooks. When the two parts are pressed together the hooks catch onto the plush loops and form a firm grip. It can be easily separated by a firm pull outwards – never downwards from below. Because the Velcro is sewn along the top edge of a hanging it can take the weight evenly over the entire width of the piece. It is also helpful in hanging uneven pieces and is less damaging to textiles than older methods. Velcro can be bought in many different widths to cope with all weights of fabric. The part which goes on the batten can be stapled to it; it does not need to be stuck. And the batten can have holes along the top edge for suspension cords.

It is usually safer to display small items in a case. If a suitable one is not available then improvise by making one from an old drawer and fixing it to a wall or a table top. If it is to go on a table then you will probably need some glass to protect the items, but if it is on a wall out of reach then this may not be necessary.

Fan collectors often have specially shaped cases made for their best pieces. These afford protection and support and if a fan is lent in one of these it should not be removed. Others are sometimes displayed in a box, using an old picture frame as the border. These cases are not often glazed but merely used to show off the fan temporarily.

Good ideas will come to you as you visit museums, exhibitions or collectors' homes. Each new display will demand slightly different solutions as the room available and the time at your disposal limit the options.

WEARING COSTUME

On the whole most serious costume collectors and museum curators would prefer not to see period clothing worn, but there can be the odd occasion when it is justified. Occasional wearing, if certain precautions are taken, is not necessarily going to be bad, but the use of a collection for fashion shows will not be good for the pieces. The clothes cannot stand up to the demands of a show where the models have to change quickly. They do not usually have time to change their underwear to give the clothes the correct shape, and very often the fastenings have to be modified by adding zip fasteners or some other easier method so that the models can get in and out of them quickly. It is very rare for a show of this kind to give the audience a good idea of how old clothes looked when worn, and defeats the whole purpose of doing it in the first place.

When selecting a dress to wear from her collection the collector should first of all make sure that the one she chooses is going to be strong enough. Next, the person to wear the garment should be slightly smaller than the dress but of the right height. When trying on the dress always wear heels of the correct height.

Accessories

The next consideration is the accessories. The right collars, cuffs, shawls, bag, gloves, shoes, head-dress and jewellery play a major role and must be in good condition. The person who is to wear the pieces must either have her hair dressed to suit the period or use a wig. Men should be prepared to sacrifice their beards for periods when they were not fashionable.

Once all the pieces for display are assembled give some thought to the undergarments. Even if there is a suitable corset in the collection it will be better to make a reproduction one out of strong cotton and light boning, using the original as a pattern. On the other hand you may not need a corset at all. With a heavily boned 1890s' evening dress there will be enough shape in the bodice and a corset may well add an extra inch to the wearer's waist, so provided you do not strain the dress it may be easier to do without one. The bust can be forced into the correct place by taping it or wearing a modern brassière which is boned and adjustable. Any extra flesh needed can be added by padding.

A good skirt shape can be achieved by using genuine or reproduction petticoats, but take care with crinolines. If you do not put enough petticoats over the cage the frames will show through and look very ugly, particularly on a photograph where the light will show up the ridges. Brown paper can again be used as a base petticoat by pinning or taping it to a waistband, but if the skirt still

39 A velvet dress of about 1885–6 showing the bustle at its height. Photographed on a living model against a fairly simple background which allows the dress shape to stand out. *The Gallery of English Costume, Platt Hall, Manchester*

looks flat, even with a number of petticoats under it then try adding a reproduction one heavily starched.

Thick white stockings, not the thin nylon or flesh-coloured variety, should be worn, except for the periods when black stockings were preferred. The correct colour and thickness are important because nothing looks worse than seeing a 'naked' leg under a Victorian dress. Many amateur actresses do not appreciate this and as they are above audience level glimpses of flesh-coloured ankles look odd when they should be white. Do not use stockings from your collection unless absolutely necessary because perspiration discolours the feet and this is not easy to remove.

Shoes can be something of a problem. Those in your collection will probably not fit and if they do they should not be worn out of doors for any reason as they may well be damaged. As mentioned previously the Victorians often had their feet painted out of photographs, which is one way of dealing with the matter if a photograph is being taken. Reproduction shoes may not be easy to make so discreet modern ones will have to be worn, but see that the heel height conforms to the original period.

Photography

If the object of dressing up in the clothes is to take a photograph, then think about suitable backgrounds beforehand. Good weather is necessary for outdoor photography, and if you choose locations well in advance the models will not have to stand around in antique costume, which can be hot and uncomfortable.

Before any garments are worn sew dress shields inside the dress to stop underarm perspiration marking the fabric. A piece of cotton tacked inside the neckline and round the inside of cuffs will help in these areas. With a high-necked dress it is a good idea for the wearer to put on a cotton vest with a high back in case perspiration is a problem here. Cotton and not a synthetic fabric should be used, as the idea is to soak up the moisture before it gets to the dress. Men should wear a cotton shirt.

If photographs are being taken then the lighting will be quite strong, whether they are done inside a studio or outside in the sunshine. The wearer will need a certain amount of make-up as the strong light will take away the contours of the face, leaving it looking rather flat. The face should not, of course, look made up if the dress belongs to a period when make-up was not worn – the idea is merely to give some modelling to the face.

The make-up and hairstyle must be done before putting on the dress, but take great care because make-up stains are among the worst kind to remove. Some sort of protection, such as a large scarf, should be put over the head to help the hairstyle remain in place and stop make-up getting on the clothes in the first place.

It is not easy for someone who is modelling an old dress to achieve an authentic appearance. Ideally the person who knows most about costume should not be the one wearing the dress, as she should be on the spot to correct posture and stop any photograph being taken which looks out of period. Some of the best photographs of live models wearing antique costume are to be found in the excellent series of booklets produced by the Gallery of English Costume, Platt Hall, Manchester. These were taken during the years from the late 1940s to the mid-1950s and some of them could almost be mistaken for original photographs.

CHAPTER NINE

Museums, Libraries, Archives and Societies

Some collectors are quite happy just to possess objects and are not interested or even curious about the date, the history or the development of their pieces. But for those who want to discover more about their collections there are many interesting by-ways that will open up. For the costume and textile collector the field is wide open because the subject touches on a very important area of everyone's life. Although some find it hard to accept that this subject is worthy of serious study, remember that first wool and then cotton were the basis of Britain's wealth, and this is not the only country which owed its prosperity to these fibres. Whatever economic historians might write on the organisation of the textile industry and its impact on the economy of the country, a commodity was being produced which was needed or desired by someone else willing to pay for it, and it is the product which is important and deserving of attention. Economic historians write about the clothing industry as a whole but tend to ignore the clothes themselves, and this neglect means that the collector will have many questions which will go unanswered.

Research on many historical subjects is frustrated by the lack of evidence. Conversely, there are some periods when there is almost too much material and it is difficult to sort out what is important and relevant. It is easy to lose one's way in the mass of documentation available for the twentieth century, for example, and concentrate too much on the general influence of Parisian haute couture, without considering other factors which might modify that influence in local circumstances. A sense of proportion is needed.

For collectors anxious to find out more about their objects there are three public institutions which house the material culture of our past: museums hold the objects; libraries contain the books and archives conserve the manuscript sources.

MUSEUMS

Museums have had a bad press recently, partly because they are easy targets to knock and partly because there is a profound misunderstanding of their role in the world. Museums, and the term includes art galleries, are seen as fuddy-duddy, expensive anachronisms, peopled by uniformed curators who jealously guard the contents from the public.

The buildings called museums house the natural and man-made history of our culture, and as such are shrines dedicated to the remembrance of our past for the benefit of our future. They are used to underline our national pride and our pride in our inheritance as human beings. They reflect for some a better world that has gone; for others a reminder of a grim past to measure future progress by. They are shrines too to the industry of the nameless as well as the famous, the only memorial of their life that some people will ever have. Museums bring into the reach of ordinary people a microcosm of a particular era, industry, place or discipline. Not to understand something of the complex emotional needs which museums satisfy in people is to misunderstand the role the curator, as guardian, plays within the museum.

Museums are particularly disliked by some collectors who see them as rapacious in their desire to hoard objects which the collectors would like for themselves. These hoards will never be released onto the market once they are in a museum, so they are effectively taken out of circulation, which reduces the number of objects available for collectors to buy.

However, without objects museums lose their *raison d'être*. It is their primary function to acquire objects; secondly, they must house them safely so that they do not deteriorate. Once this is satisfied then means of making the objects available to the public have to be found. This is usually by displays or exhibitions, but it also includes work with schoolchildren, lectures to adults, writing about the objects in learned journals, books and catalogues, holding open days, and making provision for scholars and interested laymen to see objects in store.

In Britain there are over a thousand museums, the majority of which are publicly owned and paid for out of the rates. About twenty are national museums, paid for by taxes. Of the remainder some are owned by universities and trusts while a very few are entirely privately owned. There is no legal definition of a museum and no obligation for them to be registered anywhere. Many call themselves national museums when they are not in fact paid for by the government, and indeed may well be privately owned.

The subjects covered by the museums are vast. The majority, however, are undoubtedly county or town museums which reflect the man-made and natural history of their area, and most will have some costume and textile items. Other museums are highly specialised but will collect any textile items relevant to their subject; military or theatrical collections will obviously include a great number of costumes.

It is in the specialist departments within large museums that most of the major general collections of costume and textiles can be found. These are often decorative arts departments, dealing with all the subjects other than paintings and drawings which come under the heading of arts.

The main collections of costume on display in Britain at the time of writing are to be found in the following places:

Barnard Castle, The Bowes Museum
Bath, The Museum of Costume, Assembly Rooms
Brighton, Museum and Art Gallery
Cardiff, The Welsh Folk Museum, St Fagan's
Edinburgh, The National Museum of Antiquities of Scotland
    The Royal Scottish Museum – which also operates the Shambellie
    House Museum of Costume, at New Abbey, near Dumfries
Nr Exeter, Killerton House (National Trust)
Nr Kidderminster, Hereford & Worcester County Museum,
    Hartlebury Castle
Leicester, Costume Museum, Wygston's House
London, Bethnal Green Museum of Childhood
    The Museum of London
    Victoria and Albert Museum (costume galleries due to re-open in
    1983)
Manchester, Gallery of English Costume, Platt Hall
Northampton, (shoe collection) Central Museum of Art Gallery
Nottingham, Museum of Costume & Textiles, Castlegate
Paisley, (shawl collection) Museum and Art Gallery

Worthing, Worthing Museum and Art Gallery
Nr York, Castle Howard Costume Galleries
York, Castle Museum

The Costume Research Centre, 4 The Circus, Bath, is an extension of the Museum of Costume and provides study facilities and an enquiry service for students, research workers and the public. There is a library with books, periodicals, fashion plates, photographs and other documentary sources, as well as a study collection of costumes and accessories.

Many other museums have large costume collections, for example Glasgow City Museum, but lack space to display it permanently. There are a great many more which have a small gallery or some cases with costume.

Before going to see any costume on display check that the gallery or museum is open. Recently several museums have had to close on certain days of the week, or even for whole months in the winter, because of economic stringencies. At any time there may be closures for maintenance or because of staff sickness, resulting in an inadequate number of security personnel to keep parts of a museum open. Costume displays are also subject to frequent change in order to protect the pieces.

One category on the increase is that of a costume collection attached to a country house. These are usually privately owned, the largest being at Castle Howard, near York. Killerton House, near Exeter, has a collection now run by the National Trust which also owns the Charles Wade Collection at Snowshill Manor, now temporarily moved to Blickling Hall, Norfolk, for conservation reasons.

The only book which lists in detail the scope of the collections in museums is *Handbook of Costume* by Janet Arnold. This is now very out of date but a revision is promised. Museums generally are listed in a yearly publication called *Museums and Galleries in Great Britain and Ireland*, which also indexes them very briefly by collection. Historic houses appear in a companion booklet called *Historic Houses, Castles and Gardens of Great Britain & Ireland*. The National Trust and the National Trust for Scotland list their properties in handbooks but do not generally mention the contents. Most house owners are not particularly aware of the importance of their textile collections, as opposed to the paintings and furniture, so this information is very hard to come by.

In America there is a fascinating display at the Brooklyn Museum,

New York. Here a series of figures dressed in costumes and arranged chronologically are slowly moved in front of the visitor, who is seated in a darkened theatre. The figures are mounted on a moving belt and the show is started at a set time each day. It is probably the only moving fashion show of static figures in the world and seeing it is a rather eerie experience.

Whilst it has no permanent costume gallery, the Museum of the City of New York shows part of its extensive collection by dispersing it through the period rooms. It also has some special exhibitions, and recent ones have included the 1880s and fancy dress.

Also in New York is the Costume Institute at the Metropolitan Museum of Art. It has a fantastic collection of its own but no permanent display. Instead it mounts very large exhibitions on a different theme each year from December to late summer, which usually necessitate extensive borrowing from public and private collections round the world.

A collection which is particularly good for twentieth-century couture clothes is at the Fashion Institute of Technology in New York. This is primarily for students at the Institute and there is no display, but there are usually exhibitions each year.

Outside New York there are many very fine and extensive collections but not many permanent displays. In Canada the Royal Ontario Museum, Toronto, will shortly be opening galleries in its new extension and showing some of the marvellous pieces from its costume and textile collections. Again, before a visit check up about the contents of the museum galleries and their hours of opening. For information on foreign museums and their addresses the book by Kenneth Hudson and Ann Nicholls, *The Directory of Museums* (2nd ed., 1981), is useful.

In Europe there are several very good collections of costume and textiles which are part of large national or state collections. There are two very well-known separate costume museums which are readily accessible, one in Paris – La Musée de la Mode et du Costume in the Palais Galliéra – and the other at The Hague in the Netherlands – Het Nederlands Kostuum-Museum.

Most museums are willing to show visitors items not on display, provided they have enough staff to do this and it is compatible with the safety of the objects. A vague request to 'see the costume collection' is not generally going to open any doors very quickly. It is essential for the visitor to know fairly precisely what she wants to see. Without a published catalogue this is difficult, although some museums may well allow access to the card index if it does not contain confidential information. If the interest is in some area where a collection is unlikely to have a great many pieces, muffs for example, there will be few problems. For wider groups of material, though, it is a good idea to narrow it down, perhaps by asking to see evening dresses of the 1890s. If it is her local museum's collection which a collector is requesting to see, then she can always ask to come back and see further pieces. It is a good idea not to ask to see too many pieces at one visit; six is probably the maximum that anyone can look at comfortably at one session.

Make appointments to see items not on display well in advance as staff will have to get the things out of store. This may well take an hour or so as the locations of the pieces will have to be looked up first. When a piece is as well stored as costume ought to be, it takes time to get it out of its cocoon and it also takes time to put it back again. If you cannot keep an appointment for any reason then notify the museum as soon as possible – it is discourteous not to. Most visits have to be made during office hours on weekdays, as security restrictions often prohibit visitors to non-displayed material at the weekend. For the same reason visitors should be prepared to have a member of staff with them all the time and they will not be allowed unrestricted access to the stores.

Make sure that you have such necessary items as pencils, rubbers, paper and tape measure. Only pencils should be taken near a textile; never use a fountain pen, biro or felt-tip pen. Permission should be asked beforehand if you want to take a pattern, as this means that the piece will be handled more than it would be by normal viewing. Photographs can usually be taken for a collector's own use but must not be published without permission and the payment of a repro-duction fee. Acknowledgment should also be made if any photo-graphs or drawings of items in the museum are published.

Many museums in London are overwhelmed by visitors to the stored collections and therefore have to limit the number and time allotted to this. Museums outside London are generally less inten-sively used, often because they lack the space and staff to offer this service in the same way that London museums do. In the present economic climate this state of things is unlikely to improve, which is very frustrating for both the museums and their visitors.

Museums are allowed to identify but not to value pieces; valua-tion can only be obtained from trained valuers. Many museums will not supply written identifications now because some dealers have been unscrupulous in their use of letters from staff, often attaching a letter identifying a genuine piece seen by the curator to an inferior piece which was not seen. Some will allow items to be left for identification; others have no space to keep things and ask visitors to make appointments. It is not a good idea to send photographs of costume pieces as it can be very difficult to give an opinion from an illustration, nor should pieces be sent through the post unless the museum has indicated that this is acceptable to them. Museums will not usually recommend a particular shop, dealer or auction house as this lays them open to accusations of taking a reward for their recommendations.

LIBRARIES

Libraries in Britain are divided into two categories – reference and lending. The main reference libraries are the six copyright libraries, that is those which are allowed by law to demand a copy of every book, magazine, newspaper or piece of printed material produced in Britain. They are: the British Library; the National Libraries of Scotland and Wales; the Bodleian, Oxford; the University Library, Cambridge and Trinity College, Dublin. These libraries never lend any of their books; they exist purely for reference purposes.

Unlike museums, libraries are a statutory obligation on the local authorities in Britain. Most major library authorities run by local government have a main reference library, often with special collections connected with their area or the industries in it. They also have lending sections which can be found in most towns. Through these lending libraries it is possible to borrow books from the main lending library in the country, the British Library Lending Division at Boston Spa. Books from this library, though, may well not be allowed out of the borrowing library, depending on the rarity of the work. Books can also be borrowed via the inter-library loan network abroad.

Many universities will also allow bona fide students, or people engaged in research, to use their libraries and sometimes to borrow from them. Some of these have very specialised collections, either based on gifts or connected with the courses that they run. Also worth inquiring about are the libraries of Art Colleges, or faculties of art and design in Polytechnics, particularly those which have fashion or textile courses. They may well take some of the trade magazines which are difficult to find elsewhere. In particular, the Liddell Hart Fashion Archive at Liverpool Polytechnic is a good source.

Most museum libraries exist for the use of the staff only but they may possibly allow visitors to use them during office hours, though not to borrow books. The exception is the Victoria and Albert Museum's library which is the National Art Library and is for reference only.

The copyright libraries are the most useful source for runs of women's magazines. However, the British Library, which has the largest number of these, suffered many losses in this area during the war which have not yet been made good. In the past these libraries have sometimes found it difficult to make the copyright provisions apply and, as all but the British Library have to ask for the books they want, it depends on what they consider they should be collecting – not all nineteenth-century librarians viewed women's magazines as important.

There is a published list of all British periodicals which indicates where copies can be found. It is known by its initials as BUCOP (British Union Catalogue of Periodicals), but is rather out of date for its holdings of the older women's magazines. Published catalogues of many of the main libraries' holdings exist and can usually be found in a reference library. New techniques mean that many of these catalogues are now being updated on microfilm or microfiche, as it is easier and cheaper than the printing of catalogues. Knowing your way around this type of material is a great help for anyone who wants to pursue a line of research, and is essential if any serious work is contemplated. For a collector with a visual memory, though, the library catalogue can be daunting when she is used to looking along the open shelves of a lending library to find the books.

The use of library lending services is free to local ratepayers, but special services such as reserving books or borrowing them on inter-library loan require a small fee. Public libraries do not usually demand readers' tickets for their reference sections, but the copyright libraries require tickets so that they can keep a check on the users and restrict them if too many want to use their facilities. Access to museum, college and private libraries is at the discretion of the librarian or governing body.

ARCHIVES

The public holdings of archive material in Britain are found in record offices. There are also many private archives to be found in country houses, others are owned by businesses, by the descendants of famous people, or by ordinary individuals. The main records of government are housed in the Public Record Office in London, while most county towns and cities have their own record offices for official papers and material connected with their area. Often, if a family estate is being broken up, the archives and estate papers will be deposited in the local record office. Deposit means that the family can keep control of access to the papers, and of any proposed publication of material from their collection.

Some families have very good records going back hundreds of years which are meticulously kept, and include dressmakers' and tailors' bills of interest to the costume historian. Others have unfortunately suffered from fire, flood and other damage, and there are those not relevant to the costume enthusiast as they contain only deeds and other papers connected with land ownership. In the past some people kept everything they received – all their bills and letters – whilst others rarely wrote or else threw papers out as soon as they were finished with.

Some business records have been well kept for several generations; others have suffered losses over the years or been thrown out when a new owner took over. Many textile firms disposed of their archives before those interested in our industrial past were fully alive to the wealth of material which had survived. Even today firms still refuse to believe that old account books can be of any interest.

Record offices make lists of their holdings and also of private or business archives in their area. From these the costume historian can see if there are any items which might be of interest. Tailors' bills, private letters from relatives in London sending the latest fashions, journals and diaries: all afford an insight into our ancestors and their clothes. How this material can be used is illustrated by Anne Buck's *Dress in Eighteenth Century England,* and 'Two Eighteenth Century Tailors' by Stuart Maxwell in *Hawick Archaeological Society Transactions* (1972, pp. 3–29). There are many other similar items to be found in the rich holdings of British archives.

Record offices are usually open five and a half or six days a week but do check this because the recent economies have meant that, like museums, they have had to curtail their services to the public.

Because record offices house official documents which lawyers and government officials need to consult quickly it is possible to use them without an appointment. Some rarely used material may well be housed in another building, necessitating another appointment, so it is an idea to telephone beforehand to find out if what you need is readily available. For private archives on deposit permission from the owner may be needed first.

SOCIETIES

There are several specialist societies which collectors might like to know about or consider joining. Nearly all of them produce some kind of publication with useful articles of interest to collectors and hold meetings during the year. Some of the publications can be found in public libraries in Britain, but it can be harder to track down the foreign ones outside some of the larger specialist museum libraries, which do not usually allow outsiders to borrow from them.

The societies are listed alphabetically and where possible the addresses for contacting them have been given, as well as details of subscription rates. However, the majority are run by unpaid volunteer members so that addresses change from time to time when a new secretary takes over. Most societies in Britain will be listed in the *Directory of British Associations* (CBD Research Ltd) which is periodically updated. It will be found in most main reference libraries and can be used to check on the correct name and address to contact. In America the *Encyclopedia of Associations, Vol. 1, National Organisations of the US* (Gale Research Co.) should be consulted.

When writing to a society for information it is helpful to enclose a stamped addressed envelope. Societies are not publicly funded like museums but are run on members' subscriptions. Whilst they are usually happy to help any genuine enquiries, too many children doing projects at school write expecting detailed information on their topics, which they could easily find out about had they been taught to use a library properly.

CIETA

CIETA stands for Centre International d'Etude de Textiles Anciens and is an international society based at Lyon in France. It was founded in 1954 and is heavily biased towards silk textiles, the industry associated with Lyon, but the growing interest in all periods of textile manufacture has helped, over the last few years, to widen the scope. The membership is fairly small but the society is open to all who are interested in the study of ancient textiles, i.e. those made before the complete mechanisation of weaving.

There is a general assembly every four years in a different city in Europe, where papers are read by members on any new work they have been doing. It publishes a *Bulletin du Liaison* twice a year with articles in French or English, with a résumé in the other language. Once a year it publishes in the *Bulletin* a detailed list of all new books and articles on all aspects of textiles, including lace, carpets, fabrics, costume, embroidery and conservation. Another of its useful publications is *Fabrics: a vocabulary of technical terms*, which has been produced in about seven European languages so far. Its aim is to find in all major languages a recognised term for each technical aspect of fabric production, so that there are no ambiguities in articles and books on historical textiles.

The address is 34 rue de la Charité, 69002, Lyon, France.

The Costume Society [of Great Britain]
This was founded in 1965 for all who are interested in the study of costume and its preservation. It has about a thousand members, mostly in Britain but including many from abroad, with several libraries, colleges and museums belonging to it. It is open to all on payment of an annual subscription.

The society has an annual symposium held at a different town in Britain each year, often with a theme and with various papers being read and visits to local collections. There are other meetings and study weekends during the year and an annual general meeting.

It publishes an annual journal called *Costume* which contains a mixture of articles by professional costume historians and amateurs. There are also book reviews, a list of new books, a selective list of articles from other publications which might interest members, and notes. The standard now achieved by this journal is recognised to be very high and its reputation is growing steadily. There are also occasional special publications produced, which are sometimes reprints of rare early works or longer articles of a more specialist nature.

The subscription for individual members is in the region of £8 per annum. Enquiries should be addressed to the Honorary Secretary, c/o The Royal Scottish Museum, Chambers Street, Edinburgh EH1 1JF.

The West of England branch is based on Bath and was started in 1973 to cover the area from Cornwall to Wiltshire, Dorset to Wales and Warwickshire. It meets four times a year at the Costume Research Centre, Bath. There is a subscription of £2 but members must also belong to the main Costume Society.

The Costume Society of America

Founded in 1974 following the Costume Society [of Great Britain], it has a wide and rapidly growing membership in the USA with an increasing number of regional branches. It has an annual symposium at a different city across the States and there is usually another study weekend during the year on a particular theme. There are also occasional meetings and private views in New York.

The society publishes a lively newsletter about twice a year which has book reviews, advance notice of exhibitions, and anything relevant that has caught the editor's attention. On a more serious note it publishes a yearly journal called *Dress*, containing longer articles. The reputation of this journal is growing steadily.

The subscription for individuals is about $30. The address of the society is Suite 1702, 330 West 42nd St, New York, N.Y. 10036.

The Costume Society of Scotland.

This was founded in 1967. The original intention was to form a branch of the Costume Society, but this idea was turned down by some members who felt that the society should concentrate solely on Scottish themes. However, this has not materialised and today its active lecture programme, held during the winter months in Edinburgh, reflects the whole range of costume interests. It is open to all who wish to join.

The society produces a yearly duplicated *Bulletin* containing brief articles on various topics of interest, book reviews and notes. There is an annual summer outing to a place of particular interest for its textiles.

The subscription is in the region of £5 per annum and the honorary secretary is Miss M. N. Fraser, 4 Glencairn Crescent, Edinburgh.

The Fan Circle International

The Fan Circle was founded in 1975 'to promote the interest in fans from all over the world, for the collector, the would-be collector and the merely fascinated.' It has members all over the world and covers a very popular collecting field. There are meetings in London and the provinces, special collectors' meetings, visits to private and public collections, and collaboration with museums to hold special exhibitions of fans. It publishes a *Bulletin* twice a year which contains brief articles, book reviews, notices of meetings and advertisements. The society is open to all.

The annual subscription is about £5 and the secretary is Mrs J. Morris, 24 Asmuns Hill, Hampstead Garden Suburb, London, NW11 6ET.

Gesellschaft für Historische Waffen-und-Kostümkunde

This is the oldest surviving society for the study of costume and was originally founded in 1896 for the study of arms and armour, with costume being added later. The first journal was *Zeitschrift für Waffenkunde*, published in seventeen volumes between 1897 and 1944. The society was refounded in 1951 and the second series of the journal, known as *Mitteilungen der Gesellschaft für historische Kostüm-und-Waffenkunde*, was published from 1955 to 1959.

In 1960 the third series of the journal was started, called *Waffen-und-Kostümkunde*. This is produced twice yearly and there are usually an equal number of articles on armour and costume, with book reviews as well. The articles are mainly in German but other languages are accepted. The standard of this journal is high and its contents are often important contributions to costume history.

The society normally has a meeting every two years somewhere in Germany. The journal subscription rate is about DM35, and can be obtained from Deutsche Kunstverlag Gmbh, Vohburgher Strasse 1, 8 Munich 21, West Germany.

ICOM Costume Committee

This is a specialist committee for members of ICOM, the International Council of Museums, and is only open to affiliated members or institutional nominees. It has, however, produced a *Vocabulary of Basic Terms for Cataloguing Costume – Women's Garments*, and is working on similar ones for men's and children's costume. The system was described in an article by Anne Buck in *The Museums Journal* (vol. 76, 1976–7, pp. 109–110), and collectors might find this useful for cataloguing purposes.

The Lace Guild

This was founded in 1976 'to promote the knowledge of lace, its

making, study, collecting, teaching, history and use . . .' It is basically a craft guild with the emphasis on members who make lace,
and has a large worldwide membership. It publishes a quarterly
magazine called *Lace*, which has various articles on aspects of the
craft, patterns, and advertisements from suppliers of lace requisites.

The present subscription rate is £8 a year. The membership
secretary is Mrs C. Berrow, 7 Southwood Close, Kingswinford,
West Midlands, DY6 8JL.

The Northern Society of Costume and Textiles
The northern costume society was founded in 1977 and covers the
area north of Nottingham and Chester to the Scottish borders. Its
aims are to encourage the study and preservation of costume and
textiles. Meetings are held in different venues every three or four
months. At present it does not publish a regular bulletin but aims to
publish any particularly interesting articles as they appear. The
subscription is £3 per year and the honorary secretary is Mrs A. V.
Bickley, Bolling Hall Museum, Bowling Hall Road, Bradford, BD4
7LB.

Textile and Costume History and Conservation
This is an annual journal started in 1968 – when it was called *Textile
History* – and devoted to the economic history of textiles, with
specialist papers on textile art and design. In 1982 it was renamed
and its aims and scope were enlarged. There are two issues a year.
No society is attached to this journal which is available from the
publishers, Butterworths, at £15 per year. It has reached a very high
standard over the years, and besides articles it has book reviews and
occasional bibliographies on specialised topics.

West Midlands Costume and Textiles Society
This society covers the West Midlands area. It holds three or four
meetings a year at the City Museum and Art Gallery in Birming-
ham, and there are also outings to places of interest.

There is a subscription of £2 a year for postage and a separate
charge for each meeting. Details from Mrs S. Shreeve, 5 Hawthorn
Road, Wylde Green, Sutton Coldfield, B72 1ES.

Postscript
The very first society to study costume seems to have been founded
more than a hundred years ago, in 1882. It too was called The

Costume Society: 'or Society for Promoting the Knowledge of Costume by copying and publishing Historical Costume from Contemporary Sources only.' It had a distinguished membership including ten Royal Academicians, two bishops and many antiquarians. Sadly it lasted just a year and published only ten plates of costume. Obviously the time was not right for the serious study of costume. The detailed story of this society is told in an article by J. L. Nevinson, 'Our Predecessors, 1882–3, in *Costume* (vol. 5, 1971, pp. 22–4).

Index